THE GOOD LIVING GUIDE TO

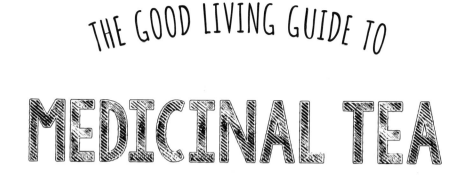

MEDICINAL TEA

50 WAYS TO BREW THE CURE FOR WHAT AILS YOU

JENNIFER BROWNE

Good Books

New York, New York

Good Books books may be purchased in bulk at special discounts for sales promotion, corporate gifts, fund-raising, or educational purposes. Special editions can also be created to specifications. For details, contact the Special Sales Department, Good Books, 307 West 36th Street, 11th Floor, New York, NY 10018 or info@skyhorsepublishing.com.

Good Books is an imprint of Skyhorse Publishing, Inc.®, a Delaware corporation.

Visit our website at www.goodbooks.com.

13

Library of Congress Cataloging-in-Publication Data is available on file.

Cover design by Jenny Zemanek
Cover photo by Wild Honey Art House

Print ISBN: 978-1-68099-061-4
Ebook ISBN: 978-1-68099-106-2

Printed in China

Acknowledgments

Thank you so much to Skyhorse Publishing, and specifically Abigail Gehring, for loving the intent and idea behind this book. Thanks for sharing in my enthusiasm and believing in my desire to find out exactly how to make medicinal teas and why they're an important alternative to conventional Big Pharma medications.

I am so grateful to have received thoughtful and patient feedback from Katolen Yardley, MNIMH, in regards to the relationship between herbs and everyday use.

A very heartfelt and sincere thanks to Tanya of Wild Honey Art House for excitedly taking beautiful photographs of tea and herbs and spices and ceramics and pottery.

I'm still sorry for breaking that dish.

And that other dish.

Lastly, thanks to Judy, Gary, Tanya, and Louise for donating an incredible variety of gorgeous props to showcase the lovely teas.

I'm a lucky girl to receive such fabulous support.

DEDICATION

For those who search for healthier alternatives and choose to question and seek honest answers.

For my mom.

burdensome or oppressive duty; to impose a rate or duty upon for or municipal purposes; burden oppress; accuse. *n.* custom, duty, impost, excise, assessment, rate.

-a-bil-i-ty (-ă-bil'i-ti), *n.* the state of being tax-

x-a-ble ('ă-bl), *adj.* subject or liable to taxation.

x-a-tion (-ā'shun), *n.* the act of taxing; rate or tax imposed; system of raising revenues; examination of a bill of costs.

x-i-cab (taks'i-cab), *n.* a motor cab of recent invention, having a mechanical device for registering time and distance traversed, the rate of fare being based on these.

x-i-der-mist ('i-dĕr-mist), *n.* one who is skilled in taxidermy.

ax-i-der-my ('i-dĕr-mi), *n.* the art of stuffing and arranging specimens of natural history.

ax-i-me-ter (taks'i-mē-tēr), *n.* an automatic device for measuring the distance travelled by a taxicab.

ax-in ('in), *n.* the resinous substance obtained from the leaves of the yew-tree.

tax-on-o-my (-on'o-mi), *n.* that department of natural history which treats of the laws and principles of classification.

taz-za (tät'să), *n.* an ornamental cup or vase with a large shallow bowl, a foot and sometimes handles. [It.]

tea (tē), *n.* the prepared leaves of the tea plant (*Thea Sinensis*); the beverage obtained by the infusion of the dried leaves; afternoon repast at which tea is served; an infusion of other substances, as beef.

teach (tēch), *v.t.* [*p.t.* & *p.p.* taught, *p.pr.* teaching], to impart knowledge to; instruct; in-

teal (tēl), *n.* a species of small, wild, fresh-water duck.

team (tēm), *n.* two or more horses, &c., harnessed to the same vehicle for drawing; litter; brood; number of persons associated together to form a side in a game, or to perform a certain piece of work.

team-ster ('stēr), *n.* the driver of

tear (tēr), *n.* a small drop of the water secreted by the lachrymal gland of the eye; anything like or similar to a tear.

tease (tēz), *v.t.* to comb, as wool or flax; separate the fibers of; irritate; annoy; vex by petty requests. *n.* one who teases.
Syn. taunt

teas-el ... which are used for ... cloth. Also ...

teat (tēt) ... male

tech-i-ly

tech-i-

techy.

tech

teah

tee

Contents

INTRODUCTION

"Tea began as a medicine and grew into a beverage."
—Okakura Kakuzō, *The Book of Tea*, 1906

My Herbal Obsession

My fascination with medicinal teas probably coincided with discovering I could solve my decade-long irritable bowel syndrome (IBS) with food. Once you experience the healing properties of plants, your eyes become wide open to the endlessly helpful possibilities of them.

Realizing that pharmaceuticals are a far cry from living nutrients forced me to take a good hard look into my medicine cabinet and question the commercialized medications I was accustomed to purchasing year after year for myself and my family. I've discovered that herbal teas can completely replace and do a better job than most of the drugs we see being advertised on our televisions or pushed by our family doctors.

Some of the more common medications one can trade for herbal teas include commercialized analgesics, anti-inflammatories, anti-nausea medications, laxatives, cough drops, and cough syrups. I'm sure many readers can agree that these medications are desired and necessary every now and then, but by using the correct herbs in the proper dosage, we can make our own medicinal teas that offer the same benefits as pharmaceuticals, *only better*.

A recent study conducted on natural anti-inflammatories and pain relievers concluded that "the evaluation of nutraceutical preparations with appropriately designed controlled studies has exploded in recent years. There is now a greater degree of confidence based on controlled study design and improved quality of the investigators that has strengthened positive findings found using natural compounds to treat diseases. It is important for healthcare practitioners to learn about these scientific studies to counsel patients who are taking various dietary supplements, herbs, minerals and vitamins for both disease treatment and prevention."[1]

Now that more and more doctors and health care providers are becoming attuned to the fact that medicinal herbs can heal with minimal side effects and expense, an incredible increase in the amount of peer-reviewed, scientific studies supporting practical use and positive conclusions are being published at a rapid pace. This is extremely encouraging!

Why Tea?

Quality herbal teas are ideal for treating a variety of ailments for the following reasons: they're cost effective, quickly absorbable, and contain no artificial dyes, colors, or preservatives. They're also simple to make, easy to tweak according to one's palate and personal preferences, and abundantly beneficial in so many ways.

Unfortunately, there are many commercialized tea companies that add a lot of filler to their blends and produce individual portions wrapped in bleached tea bags, so the responsibility falls on each of us, the consumers, to be mindful of this. By requesting labels and executing our own research, we reap huge rewards when it comes to the quality of our concoctions that ultimately determine our health outcomes.

It is important to urge pregnant women, nursing mamas, and anyone with known herbal allergies to be cautious and consult an herbalist prior to drinking medicinal teas in order to be certain to avoid any possible interactions and unfavorable side effects, but it should also be noted that prescription medications that are typically deemed safe are *not* the best solutions to most of our health problems. Exploring medicinal teas as an alternative to commercial drug preparations is often a wise choice!

Many opponents of herbal medicine cite lack of research or proof of effectiveness as a reason to abstain, but the reality is that conventional antibiotics aren't as resilient as they once were due to overuse and bacterial recognition. Many popularly prescribed pharmaceuticals contradict one another, and the number of deaths per year in the United States that are directly related to improperly administered and prescribed medication is astounding. It is time to reintroduce a safer way of treating illness—one that has been around for much longer than modern-day medicine: herbal tea.

In conducting hundreds of hours of peer-reviewed research while writing this book, I came across thousands of studies that concluded medicinal herbs have countless health benefits. There are close to five hundred of those studies cited in the references section of this book—and I certainly didn't record every abstract or journal entry that I came across.

> According to the 2014 Market Report conducted in part by the American Botanical Council, the recent rise in herbal tea sales "is indicative of a growing interest in using readily obtainable botanicals to enhance personal wellness and self-care regimens."[2]

The world is changing. We're opting to label genetically modified food and purchase organically grown produce. We're turning to herbalists, naturopaths, and compound pharmacists instead of general practitioners for holistic advice on our medical ailments. The number of natural products on grocery store shelves is growing rapidly, and we are quickly becoming aware of the unfortunate reality surrounding the current state of our health care system. We are realizing that we have to be our own best advocates when it comes to our health and that we have a *choice* in regard to how we treat our various medical issues.

Why *This* Book?

I want to be clear: I am not an herbalist, and I don't have any background in medicine. I was (and still am) curious about the subject matter of this book, and I know others are, too. I spent a lot of time researching, purchasing, and preparing herbal teas, so I could speak from experience. I consulted a licensed, currently practicing medical herbalist, who helped me a great deal when it came to getting my facts straight, and my intent for communicating what I've learned is pure. My goal when writing this book was to create a guide that is extremely easy to follow, informative, interesting, and simple to navigate. Above all, I wanted to share a wealth of knowledge on the subject of medicinal teas and the amazing ways in which they naturally heal.

This book has been divided into three main sections. Part One (Tea Tales) consists of tea-making basics. It offers measurements, tips for storage, and suggestions regarding dosage and herbal interactions. Part One also includes a list of terms that are used to describe a plant's medicinal values.

Part Two (Powerful Plants) is comprised of fifty traditional herbs: medically helpful roots, barks, flowers, leaves, seeds, and fruit. Presented alphabetically, this section discloses both their English and Latin or Greek names, medicinal uses, health benefits, and any known cautions that may be associated with them when ingested in tea form.

Part Three (50 Teas for 50 Common Ailments) is divided into three sub-sections: Acute, Chronic, and Random + Preventative. Common complaints and conditions that can be greatly helped by medicinal tea (and thoughtful, tailored recipes for each) are organized alphabetically in these pages.

There are hundreds of common ailments and disorders that we routinely take medications for. Instead of prescription drug administration, I'm offering holistic alternatives to a variety of these conditions—ones that are pure and natural, tried and true: simple medicinal teas made from fifty different species of plants and water.

That's it: *plants and water.*

Here's the bottom line: if you take multiple medications to treat a chronic illness or disease and would like to try a more holistic approach, then read this book. If you're curious about using herbs preventatively or for part of a treatment plan against diseases like cancer and Alzheimer's, then read this book. If you're like me and millions of other parents out there, and you *loathe* the idea of inducing your six-year-old to swallow artificially-colored cough syrup for her sore throat, then please read this book.

Many of the healing plants discussed are in your kitchen right now. There are herbs for fevers, bowel disease, worms, and lice. Teas included in this book provide relief for asthma, migraines, and constipation. Learn how to use herbs as medicine, clean out your conventional pharmaceutical stash, and cure what ails you one cup of tea at a time, naturally.

PART ONE: TEA TALES

"The 'art of tea' is a spiritual force for us to share."
—Alexandra Stoddard

The History of Tea

Tea has a long and interesting history. When people think of traditional tea, they're probably thinking of *Camellia sinensis*, the intoxicatingly versatile plant discovered over four thousand years ago in China (arguably). This plant was (and still is) revered for its scent and taste but most of all for its obvious health benefits. When Camellia sinensis is brewed fresh, the result is green tea, which is one of the natural remedies discussed in this book. When the leaves are fermented and then brewed, the result is either oolong (if brewed slightly fermented) or black tea (if brewed fully fermented). Although the singular plant that leads to the creation of all three teas is purportedly native to China, green tea is cultivated mostly in Japan while black and oolong are more common in Europe and India.

While green tea is discussed in this book because of its fantastic health benefits, it's typically not considered an "herbal tea." Most herbal teas are contrastive from the traditional teas brewed from Camellia sinensis because they come from a massive variety of very different plants (ones that are usually thought of as food!) and have distinct and exceptional medicinal uses.

The term "herb" is derived from the Latin word *herba*, meaning "grass." The term has been applied to plants of which the leaves, stems, or fruit are used for food, for medicines, or for their scent or flavor. Herbal medicine refers to folk and traditional medicinal practice based on the use of plants and plant extracts for the treatment of medical conditions.[3]

Although you may read about plants that are usually thought of as food (such as cranberry and lemon), to an herbalist, an herb is any plant that can be used to help and/or heal.

Other beverages may also be beneficial and delicious, but tea is what we instinctively reach for when we are sick, need emotional comfort, or are stuck staring out a window on a wet, rainy day. Tea is not only something that nourishes and provides medicinal assistance, and it's not just a lifestyle or a trendy drink of the moment. Throughout history, tea has been an integral part of millions of lives worldwide and continues to be favored as a drink of comfort. We innately know that tea can help us through sickness and health, good days and bad—and that is why this book will prove helpful to you.

Allopathic versus Traditional Philosophy and Research

When I commenced working on this book, I began to research and write from a different perspective than what the book is written and presented in now. Thankfully, a very patient medicinal herbalist pointed out to me that conclusions obtained from a test tube in a laboratory would show wildly different results than what one might exhibit from drinking tea in real life. I was citing a lot of scientific abstracts that concluded parsley would be unsafe to consume during pregnancy and that too much goldenseal would interact greatly with blood pressure medication. The kind herbalist agreed that if these herbs were concentrated to five hundred times what they might ever be in tea, then the corresponding results could possibly occur. However, it's wildly unrealistic to think anyone would ever drink four hundred gallons of parsley tea in a day, so the herb is actually safe for everyday ingestion.

I came to realize that this miscommunication found between allopathic (alternative) use and traditional (scientific) use is exactly what professionals within the alternative medicine paradigm fight throughout their careers. It's frustrating to have a patient or layperson quote the negative results of a study they've read when herbal practitioners know the particular herb is indeed safe in tea form.

Because of this common misperception, I've discovered that it's always incredibly important to note concentration levels of the herb in question. Some forms are extremely concentrated—one only needs a few drops of essential oil added to a bath to be surrounded by the overwhelming scent of lavender or eucalyptus. All essential oils are cleansing—they're antibacterial, antiviral, and kill germs on contact. Herbal extracts make fabulous natural household cleaners . . . but parsley tea? Not so much.

Herbal teas are made from dried herbs and water—they are diluted. Again, the vast majority of them are safe for everyone.

Custom Concoctions

You can certainly purchase teas that have been pre-packaged for you, but not every person is the same. We have different lives, live in different geographical locations around the world where different medicinal herbs are available to us, suffer from different ailments, and think and feel differently. We have different hopes, dreams, aspirations, and talents. Our family dynamics are different, our education is different, and we all have a very different genetic composition.

Our incredible diversity is the one thing we have in common.

That is why we all can reap huge rewards for creating our own tea. Tea that is lifestyle-specific and customized to our current health, wants, and needs. Perhaps you're an athlete looking for ways to increase performance and speed up recovery. Maybe you're a new mama who is searching for a natural way to stimulate lactation. Or perhaps you're suffering from an ailment that you're uncomfortable taking prescription medication for. Mother Nature has provided a healing plant for just about anything and everything; and tea is the vehicle for which these herbs can be permitted to do what they're intended to—*heal*.

Simples and Blends

In tea-making, the term "simple" means *one*. If you're brewing a simple, it means you're only using *one* herb and water (and maybe some honey or lemon for added flavor). Blends refer to the mixing or *blending* of herbs—using more than one. Common simple examples include chamomile or peppermint tea. Common blend examples include mixed berry tea or tea that helps you fall peacefully asleep (typically comprised of hops, chamomile, rosehips, or any other herb that lends to calmness and relaxation).

When test-driving a new herb, it's always recommended you begin with a simple. This will allow your body to react to that particular ingredient, which will in turn enable you to decide whether you like it or not and determine if you can feel a difference while drinking it. Just as with a food allergy, the best way to let your body respond to the tea is to isolate one ingredient at a time and observe any reaction, whether it be favorable or not. If you skip the testing of the simple and just brew a blend, then have a negative reaction to an ingredient, you won't know which herb to swap out in your next tea mixture.

The rule is this: simples first, blends second.

Dosing Tea

When brewing traditional black, white, or green tea, it's usually recommended you only steep for two to four minutes, but herbal tea is very different.

Here's the deal: each serving of tea consists of approximately half to one tablespoon of dried herbs—fruit, flowers, bark, leaves, stems, and/or roots—steeped (while covered) for ten to fifteen minutes in eight ounces of hot water, then strained. This is considered the "dosage." If you prefer weaker tea, use only half a tablespoon; if you prefer stronger, use a full one.

To make medicinal tea in bulk, which is a major time-saver and just all-around more practical, combine four tablespoons of dried herbs with enough boiling water to fill a one-quart glass jar or other type of container (a French press works very well). This should yield four cups of strong tea. Let steep, then strain and drink throughout the day, reheating as necessary.

When you create your own blends, the simplest way to be sure you have the correct amounts of each herb is to use "parts." For instance, if you are using chamomile, lemon balm, and lavender, you could prepare a blend consisting of two parts (two tablespoons) chamomile, one part (one tablespoon) lemon balm, and one part (one tablespoon) lavender. That way, you can make your favorite blends ahead of time, and make your tea as you go.

Dosing for Children

Medicinal tea dosage varies with age. If an adult dose is one cup, here's the rule for kiddies:

- Under 2 years: ½ to 1 teaspoon of tea
- 2–4 years: 2 teaspoons of tea
- 4–7 years: 1 tablespoon of tea
- 7–12 years: 2 tablespoons of tea[4]

Storage

Although there are many opinions regarding several steps to tea making, storage is one topic every tea connoisseur can agree on. Dried herbs are fragile, and storing them incorrectly can affect the taste and aroma of your tea. Tea is sensitive to odors, moisture, and light, so it's important to follow proper storage instructions.

Store your herbs in opaque, airtight, glass containers, in a cool, dark place. Never keep them in plastic, transparent containers, and be sure to never purchase teas from anyone who may store them this way—your tea could be ruined before you even get a chance to take it home!

Purchasing Dried Herbs

You can purchase your tea ingredients in bulk as loose, dried herbs or by the ounce from tea specialty shops. Just remember to read about the tea or herb company, and ask to see ingredient labels. Not all teas are created equal, and you don't want to consume medicinal teas that aren't pure and natural. Organic herbs that are produced honestly and mindfully are the very best. In fact, consider growing, harvesting, and drying your own herbs! It's fun, and the smell is heavenly—something you definitely don't want to miss out on.

Harvesting Tips and Tricks

Leaves

When: Harvest before the plant fully blooms—when the leaves look strong, colorful, and healthy.

How: Lay leaves in a single layer on a cookie sheet, or hang upside down somewhere safe, and place in warm temperatures with minimal humidity, good airflow, out of direct sunlight, and away from animals and insects. Once dried, store in a cool, dark place in a glass container.

Roots

When: Dig up in the fall or early spring, so they remain concentrated in their nutrients.

How: Hang in a space where they will be warm with minimal humidity, good airflow, and out of direct sunlight. Once dried, they can be chopped (for easy storage) and stored in a cool, dark place in a glass container.

Flowers

When: Pluck buds off stems just as they are beginning to open.

How: Lay flowers in a single layer on a cookie sheet, and place in warm temperature, with minimal humidity, good airflow, and out of direct sunlight. Once dried, store in a cool, dark place in a glass container.

Iced Teas

Consuming cold tea can be a fabulous way to continue your quest for good health into the summer months when hot teas may not be as desirable. Some teas, such as those brewed for diarrhea relief, work *better* when consumed cold. Here's the low-down on cold teas: brew with hot water for one minute longer than you would normally, then pour the strained tea over a shaker filled with ice and allow two minutes to cool. Garnish with fruit and/or additional herbs and enjoy! For example, if brewing cold peppermint tea, you may choose to garnish with fresh mint leaves. Similarly, rosehip tea could be garnished with a few pretty petals.

Interactions

Interaction is a term used to explain what happens when "the effect of one drug is altered by the presence of another drug(s), food or drink."[5] In herbal medicine, as in all types of medicine, interaction is a possibility that must be acknowledged. Although many interactions can be relatively harmless (such as simple ineffectiveness), some interactions between herbs and/or pharmaceuticals can be quite serious. Sometimes it is advised that herbs are not to be taken in conjunction with blood thinning medications, as is the occasional case with anise and fenugreek; some herbs, such as marshmallow and slippery elm, coat the lining of the stomach and may prevent other medications from being absorbed.

It's very important that, if you're considering taking medicinal herbs in conjunction with *any* prescription drug(s), you know and understand the possible interactions that may occur. For this reason, I highly recommend speaking to a medicinal herbalist before drinking medicinal tea if you are currently on other medication(s). Think of medicinal herbs as Mother Nature's medicine: if you are already taking conventional pharmaceuticals, you might be doubling up or creating an undesirable outcome by taking both.

In the description of each and every one of the fifty herbs featured in this book, a caution will be listed if the herb in tea form is known to interact with any substance or any circumstance. Please consult for safety reasons before brewing any of the tea recipes. Know what you're drinking, and you will reap the most rewards from your journey into the world of medicinal teas.

Glossary of Common Medical Terms

Adaptogen: a natural substance used in herbal medicine to normalize and regulate the systems of the body.

Analgesic: pain-relieving.

Antiaging: effective in slowing or stopping the effects of aging.

Antiallergenic: non-aggravating to an allergy and unlikely to cause an allergic reaction.

Antibacterial: destructive to or inhibiting the growth of bacteria.

Antibiotic: chemical substances (such as penicillin) produced by various microorganisms and fungi, which have the capacity to inhibit the growth of or to destroy bacteria and other microorganisms; used primarily in the treatment of infectious diseases.

Anti-candidal: a medicine or herb used to treat candida (yeast) conditions.

Anticonvulsant: an agent used to treat epileptic seizures.

Antiemetic: a substance or agent that suppresses nausea and/or vomiting.

Antifungal: inhibiting the growth of fungi.

Antihistamine: a substance that inhibits the production of histamines in the body; used especially for colds and allergy relief.

Anti-inflammatory: acting to reduce certain signs of inflammation, such as swelling, tenderness, fever, and pain.

Antimicrobial: destructive to or inhibiting the growth of microorganisms.

Anti-parasitic: killing or inhibiting growth of parasites.

Antipyretic: relieving or preventing a fever.

Antirheumatic: helps to relieve occurrences and symptoms of rheumatism.

Antispasmodic: helps to prevent and relieve muscle spasms and cramping.

Antitoxic: a substance or agent that counteracts toxins within the body.

Aperient: possessing a purgative or laxative affect.

Aphrodisiac: a food, drug, potion, or other agent that arouses sexual desire.

Aromatic: fragrant; smells good.

Astringent: a substance that contracts the tissues and/or passageways of the body, thereby decreasing discharges of mucus or blood.

Bronchodilator: a substance or agent that acts to dilate constricted bronchial tubes to assist breathing.

Cleanser: a substance or agent that cleans and purifies within the body.

Cooling: reducing heat (fever) and inflammation within the body.

Demulcent: an agent, often mucilaginous, that soothes and protects an irritated mucous membrane.

Deobstruent: has the ability to dislodge an obstruction.

Depressant: possessing the sedative quality of depressing or lowering vital activities.

Detoxifier: a substance or agent that rids one of poisons and/or toxins, or the effects of such.

Diaphoretic: produces perspiration.

Diuretic: increasing urine excretion.

Emmenagogue: a substance or agent that promotes menstruation.

Emollient: having a softening and/or relaxing effect.

Estrogenic: promoting or producing estrogen.

Expectorant: promoting the discharge of phlegm or other fluid from the respiratory tract.

Galactogogue: an herb that promotes, stimulates, and/or increases lactation.

Hypotensive: blood pressure reducing.

Laxative: a substance that relieves constipation.

Mucilaginous: works to create a protective layer of mucous-like substance that particular organs and/or body parts may benefit from, such as the lungs and intestines.

Nervine: relieving for nerve disorders; soothing the nerves.

Pectoral: lung-strengthening.

Purgative: a cathartic medicine or agent; stimulating waste evacuation from the bowels.

Rejuvenator: a substance used to restore or make young again.

Relaxant: an herb or drug that relaxes; especially one that lessens strain in muscle(s).

Resolvent: a remedy that decreases swelling and/or inflammation.

Sedative: a substance that calms and/or soothes.

Stabilizer: prevents deterioration or the loss of desired properties.

Stimulant: something that quickens the functional activity of some organ or part.

Stomachic: beneficial to the stomach; aids in digestion and/or increases appetite.

Styptic: an agent or substance that contracts organic tissue and stops bleeding or hemorrhage.

Toner: a substance or agent that strengthens and improves certain parts of the body.

Tonic: a healthy substance that strengthens or invigorates.

Vulnerary: promotes the healing of tissue.

PART TWO: POWERFUL PLANTS

"Would you like an adventure now, or shall we have our tea first?"
—*Peter Pan*

Knowledge is Power

In this book, you'll find some of the plants to be familiar. However, a lot of them may not be unless you're a health store frequenter or an herb junkie. (And it's definitely okay if you are.)

Regardless of what you already know and what you may not, the following section will ensure that you're well-informed by the time you're finished reading it. Careful consideration has been made to research every claim that is made about every ingredient, and sources are included at the end of this book in the references section. If you would like to learn more about the following powerful plants, please find the associated citation, and continue your search for increased knowledge.

I want to stress the importance of choosing organic products with clearly stated ingredients to make your teas. You will be soaking various plants in hot water for the purpose of optimum absorption and subsequent healing. If your plants have been sprayed with pesticides, you will be *ingesting and absorbing* all of it, which will require you to need a whole new kind of tea. Please be mindful of this as you purchase your products, and make certain you find organic ingredients.

Enjoy!

50 Medicinal Herbs

"You can never get a cup of tea large enough or
a book long enough to suit me."
–C. S. Lewis

Remember that some herbs have known drug-herb interactions and/or are not recommended under certain circumstances. Please note the safety cautions associated with them at the end of the description.

Anise

Anise can be used as a stimulant or diuretic; it is antimicrobial, antiviral, and antifungal.[6] It is also carminative, aromatic, and analgesic.[7] Anise is native to Egypt, Greece, and Turkey.

Scientific name: Anisum pimpinella

Part used: seed

Medicinal uses:

- Eases dry, bronchial, and asthmatic coughs
- Soothes the digestive tract[8]
- Aids menopause symptoms[9]

BILBERRY

Bilberry tea is fabulous for inhibiting bacterial growth in the gut. Drink while vacationing to ensure intestinal stability and ward off digestive distress due to contaminated food and water[10]—doing this may replace the need for pre-travel inoculation! It has also been shown to naturally increase insulin production and decrease blood sugar levels.[11] Bilberry is native to Europe and Asia.

Scientific name: Vaccinium myrtillus

Part used: fruit, leaf

Medicinal uses:

- Treats diarrhea
- Helps soothe eyestrain
- Aids Type-2 diabetes (non-insulin dependent)
- Decreases throat inflammation

BLACK COHOSH

Black cohosh is analgesic and a phytoestrogen, which means it can greatly help relieve menopause symptoms and premenstrual syndrome.[12] It is native to eastern Canada and the United States.

Scientific name: Cimicifuga racemosa

Part used: root

Medicinal uses:

- Painkiller[13]
- Regulates menses
- Treats menopause
- General uterine tonic
- Reduces inflammation

Caution: If taking to improve menopause symptoms, consult with an herbalist first. Hormones need to be balanced to achieve desired results, and treating oneself with a phytoestrogenic herb carelessly can be counter-productive. Also, low-dose is the rule with black cohosh. Don't over-medicate; this herb is strong. Avoid if pregnant, breastfeeding, have a known hormone-sensitive condition (such as uterine or breast cancer), experience chronic headaches, or are taking blood pressure lowering medication.[14]

Burdock

Burdock is high in protein and creates positive health changes in the body when used on a consistent basis. It's a fabulous herb for athletic recovery[15] and is antibacterial and antifungal. This herb is native to Europe and England.

Scientific name: Arctium lappa

Part used: root

Medicinal uses:

- Cleans the blood[16]
- Lowers blood sugar[17]
- Improves digestion[18]
- Natural, mild laxative
- Kills bacteria and fungus
- Reduces fevers[19]
- Treats uric acid build-up
- Prevents lactic acid build-up
- Cleanses glands
- Fights infection

Chamomile

Chamomile is gentle yet effective. Aside from being a very pretty flower, it's also a natural sedative,[20] antispasmodic, anti-inflammatory,[21] and antibacterial.[22] Chamomile is native to the United States.

Scientific name: Chamaemelum nobile

Part used: flower

Medicinal uses:

- Mild tranquilizer[23]
- Pain relieving[24]
- Stress reducing[25]
- Reduces inflammation[26]
- Helps fight infections
- Bronchial relaxant
- Relieves nausea

Caution: If symptoms of hay fever appear, discontinue use.[27]

Cinnamon

Cinnamon tea is analgesic, anti-inflammatory,[28] antiviral, and antifungal. This spice is great to warm up with and is a fabulous flavor-enhancer, often used in baking and cooking. It's native to Bangladesh, India, Sri Lanka, and Burma.

Scientific name: Cinnamon zeylanicum

Part used: bark

Medicinal uses:

- Digestive aid[29]
- Anesthetic
- Kills harmful bacteria

CRAMP BARK

Cramp bark is anti-inflammatory, antispasmodic, astringent, a muscle relaxer,[30] and a sedative. It's native to northern Asia and Europe.

Scientific name: Viburnum opulus

Part used: bark

Medicinal uses:

- Relieves abdominal pain, cramps, bloating, backache, and fluid retention[31]
- Calms the cardiovascular system
- Improves bladder distress
- Tones the uterus[32]

CRANBERRY

Cranberry is a powerful urinary tract tonic and a mild diuretic.[33] For urinary tract infections, try a consistent regimen of cranberry tea before resorting to antibiotics—you'll probably see (and feel!) a better result, without the side effects of prescription medication.[34] It's native to Europe, Asia, and North America.

Scientific name: Vacinnium macrocarpon

Part used: fruit

Medicinal uses:

- Treats urinary tract infections
- Relieves water retention
- Tones the bladder and kidneys

DANDELION

This little "weed" boasts some major vitamins and minerals! The root is a diuretic, liver cleanser, and detoxifier, and both the root and leaves make an excellent digestive tonic and mild laxative.[35] It's native to Europe and China, but as you probably already know, it likes to pop up *everywhere*.

Scientific name: Taraxacum officinale

Part used: root, leaf, flower

Medicinal uses:

- Natural laxative
- Helps anemia[36]
- Optimizes digestion[37]
- Aids water retention[38]
- Detoxifies joints and prevents arthritic inflammation
- Prevents cell damage from free radicals through detoxification
- Treats hepatitis and jaundice
- Stabilizes mood swings[39]
- Prostate cleansing
- Helps dissolve urinary stones

Caution: If a rash develops, discontinue use. Some people are sensitive to the milky substance that resides in the flowers and stems.[40]

Dong Quai

Dong quai is anti-inflammatory, antiviral, antifungal, antirheumatic, and antispasmodic. It's also a blood and digestive tonic, circulatory stimulant, hormone stabilizer, mild laxative, and expectorant. This plant is native to China.

Scientific name: Angelica sinensis

Part used: root, leaf

Medicinal uses:

- Eases stomach cramps and bloating
- Improves digestion
- Treats headaches and migraines[41]
- Fights viruses, bacteria, and fungus
- Improves heart health and blood circulation[42]
- Enhances concentration and memory
- Detoxifies the liver
- Restorative for muscles
- Stabilizes hormone production[43]
- Improves menopause symptoms[44]

Caution: Do not use if you have diabetes, have a clotting disorder, or are awaiting surgery.[45]

Echinacea

Echinacea is an undeniably amazing immune stimulant, which is what it's primarily used for. It's also antimicrobial, antiallergenic, antiviral, antifungal, anti-inflammatory, and diaphoretic. This plant is native to North America.

Scientific name: Echinacea angustifolia and purpurea

Part used: root, leaf, flower, seed

Medicinal uses:

- Boosts the immune system[46]
- Removes toxins
- Fights infection[47]
- Stimulates production of white blood cells and regulates red blood cells[48]
- Cleans the blood, lymph system, kidneys, and liver
- Fights bacteria, viruses, fungus, and microbes

Caution: If symptoms of hay fever appear, discontinue use.[49]

ELDER

Elder is a fantastic plant to use for respiratory nuisances. It's an expectorant, circulatory stimulant, mild laxative, and diuretic. It's native to Britain and Europe.

Scientific name: Sambucus nigra

Part used: flower, berry

Medicinal uses:

- Reduces fever and inflammation[50]
- Great for colds, flu, coughs, and general congestion[51]
- Helps with seasonal allergies and hay fever[52]

Caution: Do not consume uncooked elder berries; they may cause digestive upset.

Eucalyptus

(Eucalyptus globulus)

Although eucalyptus is an extremely beneficial herb for purifying (it's antimicrobial, antiseptic, and makes a fabulous insect repellent!), it is not fit for tea as it can be extremely toxic if ingested orally.[53] In its essential oil form, a few drops of eucalyptus can be added to steam for the purpose of cleaning contaminated air[54] and relieving respiratory issues.[55] (I've used it myself to aid my kids' coughs when croup comes calling.) It can also be used topically as a scalp rinse to rid one's head of lice.
***Lice-Be-Gone*:** Simply combine 10 drops of eucalyptus oil with ⅓ cup of olive oil, and work into the hair and scalp until completely distributed. Cover the head with a plastic shower cap, and leave on for three to four hours. Remove, and wash hair thoroughly.

Eyebright

Eyebright is a tonic, astringent, and anti-inflammatory. It's native to England, Europe, Asia, and North America.

Scientific name: Euphrasia officinalis

Part used: stem, leaf, flower

Medicinal uses:

- Healing to the eyes, nose, and throat
- Helps relieve bronchial conditions[56]
- Relieves eyestrain[57]
- Reduces hay fever symptoms

Fennel

In full plant-form, fennel reminds me of a heart with valves—it even *looks* medicinal. When making tea, we use fennel seeds, which are a circulatory tonic with an estrogenic effect. The seeds are also a diuretic, an expectorant,[58] carminative,[59] and anti-inflammatory. (And it's yummy!) It's native to the Mediterranean.

Scientific name: Foeniculum vulgare

Part used: seed

Medicinal uses:

- Aids in digestive issues[60]
- Improves the absorption of nutrients
- Eases bloating and water retention
- Excellent for sore throats and gum disorders
- Fights urinary tract infections
- Flushes toxins
- Helps relieve chest congestion[61]

Fenugreek

Fenugreek is an aphrodisiac, digestive tonic, and uterine stimulant. It's also a demulcent, anti-inflammatory,[62] and native to North Africa and India.

Scientific name: Trigonella-foenum-graecum

Part used: seed

Medicinal uses:

- Relieves indigestion and stomach upset[63]
- Lowers blood sugar[64]
- Aids in sinus (especially ear) congestion
- Treats eczema[65]

Caution: Talk to an herbalist if you wish to ingest fenugreek while taking blood-thinning medication.[66]

Feverfew

Feverfew is a uterine and digestive stimulant, expels worms,[67] relaxes blood vessels, and is anti-inflammatory.[68] It's native to Europe and Britain.

Scientific name: Chrysanthemum parthenium

Part used: leaf

Medicinal uses:

- Natural antihistamine[69]
- Clears chest congestion and phlegm
- Relieves bronchial spasms
- Prevents headaches and migraines when taken routinely[70]
- Useful for premenstrual syndrome
- Helps relieve arthritis and sciatica[71]
- Aids in expulsion of intestinal worms

Caution: Talk to an herbalist first if you wish to ingest feverfew while taking blood-thinning medication.[72]

Flaxseed

(Linum catharticum)

Flax can do more than keep you regular; it's also antirheumatic,[73] a demulcent, and a health tonic. Unfortunately, it would also make for a thick, muddled, sludge-like tea. It would be better to add ground flaxseed to a fruit smoothie to reap the rewards of both its cancer-reducing[74] and laxative effects.[75]

GINGER

Ginger is antispasmodic, antiseptic, and carminative. It's also a tonic, expectorant, and above all, a circulatory stimulant. This root is native to southern China.

Scientific name: Zingiber officinale

Part used: root

Medicinal uses:

- Increases blood flow and circulation
- Stops nausea and queasiness[76]
- Aids in relief for osteoporosis, arthritis, gout, and rheumatism[77]
- Beneficial for colds, congestion, and chills
- Lowers blood sugar and cholesterol[78]
- Prevents blood clots, thereby reducing the risk for heart attack and stroke
- Stimulates digestive enzymes
- Has an overall calming effect
- Lowers blood pressure[79]

GINKGO

Ginkgo is an herb many are familiar with. Its name means "the life enhancer." The herb is hundreds of millions of years old and was the only surviving plant in the surrounding area following the Hiroshima blast. It's antifungal, anticancer,[80] antibacterial, an astringent, a diaphoretic, and a stimulant.

Scientific name: Ginkgo biloba

Part used: leaf

Medicinal uses:

- Aids in allergies and asthma[81]
- Improves circulation[82]
- Prevents cognitive signs and symptoms of advanced aging[83]
- Helps improve memory[84]
- Can reduce symptoms of Alzheimer's disease[85]
- Contributes to prevention of genetic-associated reproductive cancers[86]

GINSENG

Like ginkgo, most people are familiar with ginseng. It's an antidepressant, an aphrodisiac, a nervine, a tonic, and an adaptogen. It's native to China, Eastern Asia, and North America but cultivated in Korea and Japan.

Scientific name: Panax (white) ginseng or Eleuthero ginseng

Part used: root

Medicinal uses:

- Stress relief
- Organ strengthening
- Assists in the treatment of Alzheimer's disease[87]
- Enhances immunity[88]
- Prevents cellular aging[89]
- Decreases fatigue[90]
- Great for adrenal health and the nervous system
- Regulates blood sugar[91]
- Fights exhaustion, depression,[92] and anxiety
- Treats lung disorders
- Helps immune system combat tumors[93]

Goldenseal

(Hydrastis canadensis)

Goldenseal is a remarkable herb with many health benefits; however, it's currently endangered, and many herbalists are avoiding it for that very reason. Although it has many medicinal uses, including healing and sealing open wounds, reducing eye, nose, and throat inflammation,[94] and killing and inhibiting the spread of bacteria and intestinal worms, it's extremely non-palatable and is difficult for even the most seasoned herbal tea consumers to drink.

Green Tea

Though it is known as Japan's national beverage, green tea is actually native to China. Green, oolong, and black tea all come from the same plant, but green tea is made from the fresh, unfermented leaves. Green tea is the strongest (medicinally) of the three. It's anticancer,[95] anti-inflammatory,[96] antibacterial, antiviral, and a stimulant.

Scientific name: Camellia sinensis

Part used: leaf

Medicinal uses:

- Protects cells from free radical damage[97]
- Lowers blood pressure and cholesterol[98]
- Regulates blood sugar
- Prevents cardiovascular disease[99]
- Immune-boosting[100]
- Mild decongestant
- Prevents tooth decay and gum disease
- Assists in wakefulness

HAWTHORN

Hawthorn is a relaxant, heart tonic,[101] astringent, diuretic, and antispasmodic. It's also hypotensive and a vasodilator. This very tall-growing tree is native to North Africa, Europe, and Western Asia.

Scientific name: Cratagus oxyacantha

Part used: fruit, flower, leaf

Medicinal uses:

- Increases circulation[102]
- Stabilizes blood pressure[103]
- Combats anemia[104]
- Tones the heart[105]

Caution: Consult with an herbalist before using hawthorn if taking heart medication.[106]

HOPS

Hops are the green cones surrounding the female flower of the hops plant. They are antibiotic,[107] antimicrobial, and antispasmodic. This herb is also liver stimulating, a diuretic, a sedative, astringent, and a blood cleanser. Hops are native to England and Europe and well known as a primary ingredient in beer. (Bet you knew *that*, already!)

Scientific name: Humulus lupulus

Part used: flower (cone and grains)

Medicinal uses:

- Aids digestion
- Natural remedy for PMS and menopause symptoms[108]
- Relieves irritable bowel syndrome (IBS), diverticulitis, colitis, and stomach ulcers[109]
- Reduces fluid retention
- Treats insomnia,[110] tension, and anxiety[111]
- Relieves pain
- Reduces fevers[112]
- Kills intestinal worms[113]

HOREHOUND (WHITE)

From the mint family, white horehound is a tonic, an expectorant, diuretic, diaphoric, deobstruent, stomachic, and resolvent. Ancient lore says this plant has the power to break magic spells! It's native to Britain.

Scientific name: Marrubium vulgare

Part used: leaf

Medicinal uses:

- Kills intestinal worms[114]
- Treats asthmatic phlegm and nagging cough[115]
- Helps wheezing, shortness of breath, and other breathing difficulties[116]

Horehound 101

There are two different species of horehound: black and white. While both types are medicinal, black horehound is less potent than the white variety and is extremely bitter. Although both varieties make great medicinal tea, black horehound often makes a better tincture.

HORSETAIL

Horsetail is prehistoric! Today it resembles grass, but back when dinosaurs were around, it grew much, much taller. It's very rich in silica, which contributes to healthy skin, hair, and nails. Horsetail is astringent, diuretic, styptic, and a tissue and kidney tonic. It's native to southern Europe.

Scientific name: Equisetum arvense

Part used: leaf

Medicinal uses:

- ❧ Stops bleeding when tea is applied topically to an external wound
- ❧ Increases bone formation[117]
- ❧ Repairs tissue[118]
- ❧ Treats bleeding ulcers, hemorrhoids, and eases menses
- ❧ Strengthens hair and nails[119]
- ❧ Aids in healthy skin
- ❧ Treats urinary tract infections and kidney stones[120]
- ❧ Reduces inflammation

LAVENDER

Aside from being incredibly beautiful and fragrant, lavender has many valuable health benefits! The purple flower is antiseptic, antispasmodic, and antibacterial. It's also an analgesic, a relaxant, and a nerve tonic. This well-known and easily identifiable herb is native to the western Mediterranean, but I'm lucky enough to have some growing in my backyard, just outside my kitchen window.

Scientific name: Lavandula officinalis

Part used: flower

Medicinal uses:

- Remedy for tension headaches[121]
- Calming[122]
- Treats insomnia
- Relieves stress, anxiety, and depression[123]

Caution: Lavender is generally considered safe, but it's recommended that pregnant women avoid drinking lavender tea in large quantities.[124]

Lemon

Lemon is antirheumatic, antibacterial, and an antioxidant. Besides making a great natural cleanser for kitchen and bath surfaces, it has many medicinal benefits. Lemon is believed to be native to Europe and India.

Scientific name: Citrus limon

Part used: fruit, peel

Medicinal uses:

- Fights infection[125]
- Kills bacteria[126]
- Aids mouth and throat infections
- Reduces fever[127]
- Detoxes the body
- Induces bowel movements[128]

LEMON BALM

Lemon balm grows wild in my backyard! It's fast-growing, fragrant, and resembles peppermint so closely that I sometimes need to smell it to be sure what it is. It's *strongly* antiviral, antibacterial, and aromatic. It's also a digestive stimulant, an antidepressant, antihistamine,[129] and nerve tonic. Lemon balm is native to southern Europe.

Scientific name: Melissa officinalis

Part used: leaf

Medicinal uses:

- Assists in allergy relief[130]
- Aids respiratory healing
- Relieves tension and anxiety[131]
- Mood lifting
- Great for stress-related disorders, such as IBS
- Calming

Caution: Lemon balm is a mild thyroid inhibitor; those suffering from low thyroid function (hypothyroidism) should take care and speak to an herbalist before using.[132]

Licorice

Licorice is anti-inflammatory, antiallergenic, anti-arthritic, and antipyretic. It's also a diuretic and a mild expectorant. Licorice is often used to add flavor to blends and is quite strong. It's native to southeast Europe and southwest Asia.

Scientific name: Glycyrrhiza glabra

Part used: root

Medicinal uses:

- Tones the adrenals, which combats stress[133]
- Detoxifies
- Reduces respiratory and joint inflammation[134]
- Clears phlegm
- Fights irritability, fatigue, and depression[135]
- Assists in concentration and nutrient absorption[136]
- Eases allergic symptoms
- Soothes indigestion[137]
- Improves ulcers[138]
- Tones the spleen

Caution: Consult with an herbalist before using if heart and/or thyroid problems, hypertension, and/or kidney disorders are present.[139]

LUNGWORT

Lungwort is emollient, demulcent, and mucilaginous. It's also an expectorant, astringent, tonic, and pectoral. It's native to the Mediterranean.

Scientific name: Pulmonaria officinalis

Part used: leaf

Medicinal uses:

- Lung and respiratory tract cleansing[140]
- Prevents disease and infection
- Protects the lungs[141]
- Helpful for allergies, asthma, wheezing, shortness of breath, and bronchitis[142]
- Cleansing for the pulmonary system

MARIGOLD

Marigold is more than a pretty plant; it's antibacterial, antiviral, antifungal, and astringent. It's also an estrogenic, and a detoxifier. Marigold is native to the Canary Islands and the Mediterranean.

Scientific name: Calendula officinalis

Part used: flower

Medicinal uses:

- ❧ Fights cancer cells[143]
- ❧ Supports liver and kidney function[144]
- ❧ Reduces inflammation[145]
- ❧ Prevents dermatitis in those receiving radiation treatment[146]

MARSHMALLOW

For my entire life, up until writing this book, I've spelled this word with an "e." Marsh*mellow*. It's antiaging, anti-inflammatory,[147] emollient, demulcent, mucilaginous, and diuretic. Marsh*mallow* is native to China and Europe.

Scientific name: Althea officinalis

Part used: root

Medicinal uses:

- Protects the respiratory tract
- Soothes intestinal lining[148]
- Treats colitis and diverticular disease[149]
- Reduces internal and external swelling[150]
- Assists in urinary tract troubles[151]
- Strengthens kidneys
- Lowers blood sugar[152]

Caution: Marshmallow root may slow the absorption of nutrients and/or other medications.[153]

More on Marshmallow

The French created the sugary treat we all know as a "marshmallow." The gummy juices of the roots were reduced and combined with eggs and sugar, to create a substance that would stop a cough in its tracks. Eventually, the roots and sugar were replaced by gelatin and corn syrup, and instead of being synonymous with medicine, marshmallow has become widely recognized as a s'more ingredient.

MILK THISTLE

Milk thistle is native to Europe. It's antiallergenic,[154] antiaging, and anti-toxin, and probably best known for being a successful liver tonic.[155]

Scientific name: Silybum marianum

Part used: seed

Medicinal uses:

- ❧ Strengthens and protects the liver from free radical damage[156]
- ❧ Aids in the treatment of viral hepatitis[157]
- ❧ Reduces damage done to liver by alcoholism
- ❧ Encourages elimination of toxins[158]
- ❧ Aids in the treatment of fatty liver disease[159]
- ❧ Combats depression[160]

Caution: Women who are pregnant or breastfeeding and those with a history of hormone-related cancers should consult with an herbalist prior to taking milk thistle.[161]

MULLEIN

Mullein is another common "weed" with tall, flowering stalks. It is antispasmodic, an expectorant, analgesic, and antiseptic, with a positive history of medicinal effectiveness. It's native to Europe, Asia, and northern Africa but also grows in North America and Australia.

Scientific name: Verbascum thapsus

Part used: root, leaf, flower

Medicinal uses:

- Expels mucus and phlegm
- Eases chest colds and bronchial irritations
- Helps relieve breathing-related allergy symptoms and respiratory stress
- Improves glandular health
- Fights infection

Caution: Take care when using externally; mullein can be irritating to the skin.[162]

NETTLE

Nettle is mostly known for its stinging quality—a plant to beware of when hiking or camping. However, it has some amazing medicinal properties! It's a circulatory stimulant, a blood tonic, antiseptic, astringent, an antidepressant, and a diuretic.[163] It grows all over the place.

Scientific name: Urtica dioica

Part used: root, leaf (primarily), seed

Medicinal uses:

- Stimulates lactation[164]
- Induces wakefulness and lends energy
- Improves aches in joints from arthritis, gout, and rheumatism[165]
- Beneficial to the urinary tract, gallbladder, and kidneys[166]
- Helps symptoms of PMS[167]
- Contains histamines to treat asthma, allergies, and hay fever[168]

Caution: Coming into contact with fresh nettle can leave a painful rash.

PARSLEY

Parsley is super easy to grow in a pot or directly in your garden. It's a natural antihistamine and mild antibiotic; it's native to the Mediterranean region.

Scientific names: Apium sativum and petroselinum

Part used: leaf, stem

Medicinal uses:

- Restores digestion[169]
- Helps modulate blood sugar levels[170]
- Helps preserve memory[171]

PEPPERMINT

Peppermint is another easy herb to grow and is *delicious* to add to water, tea, smoothies, and salads. It's antispasmodic, antiseptic, anesthetic, astringent, analgesic, and diaphoretic. It's also a tonic, decongestant, stimulant, stomachic,[172] and antiemetic.

Scientific name: Mentha piperita

Part used: leaf, flower

Medicinal uses:

- Relieves nausea and seasickness
- Helps IBS symptoms[173]
- Aids in relieving hangovers[174]
- Decreases flatulence[175]
- Numbs abdominal pain[176]
- Calms, restores, and lends clarity
- Relieves toothaches and headaches
- Clears throat and bronchial tubes[177]
- Boosts energy

Peppermint: Food or Medicine?

Good question! It depends on the dosage. Chewing on a few fresh peppermint leaves or blending some in your smoothie could definitely help lend some energy, as well as give your body a boost of calcium, but drinking three cups of peppermint tea per day throughout the duration of your first trimester of pregnancy? That could save you from morning sickness.

PLANTAIN

Not to be confused with the banana-like fruit commonly used in Central American cooking, plantain is distinguished by its green, oval-shaped leaves that grow in a rosette. Each leaf has tiny veins that run vertically, and when broken, these veins resemble celery strings.

Like dandelion and mullein, plantain is often viewed as an unwanted weed. Also like dandelion and mullein, plantain has incredible medicinal benefits! It's astringent, demulcent, cooling, detoxifying, and antiseptic. It's also a decongestant, deobstruent, expectorant, and a diuretic.[178] Plantain is native to Europe and Asia.

Scientific name: Plantago major and minor

Part used: root, leaf, seed

Medicinal uses:

- Promotes healing
- Fights infection
- Great for allergies and asthma
- Prevents mucosal infections
- Treats prostate enlargement
- Soothes and reduces pain and spasms
- Detoxifies the colon and liver

Have a splinter?

Plantain possesses excellent drawing properties, which make it highly useful for drawing out deep splinters. Simply soak the area of the splinter in hot plantain tea for half an hour. Repeat the soaking a few times throughout the day, until the splinter has moved close enough to the surface to be pulled out.

RASPBERRY

Raspberry is much more than just a welcome addition to pancakes or a spread for toast—its leaves are highly medicinal! It's a pelvic and uterine relaxant, a mucous cleanser, astringent, and toner. Who knew?! Raspberry leaf is native to Europe.

Scientific name: Rubus idaeus

Part used: leaf

Medicinal uses:

- Provides diarrhea relief[179]
- Relieves sore throat due to cold[180]
- Provides relief for symptoms associated with uterine disorders[181]
- Strengthens kidneys and urinary tract[182]

Red Clover

Red clover is a honeybee's best friend—they love it! Besides being hardy and simple to cultivate, it's also vitamin- and mineral-rich. Red clover contains phytoestrogens and, although not formally recognized, has been found to be antitumor. It's native to Europe, west Asia, and North Africa.

Scientific name: Trifolium pratense

Part used: leaf, flower

Medicinal uses:

- Aids in respiratory recuperation[183]
- Beneficial in treating menopause symptoms[184]
- Rids the body of excess estrogen, a condition which can contribute to cancer[185]

Caution: Red clover is a natural blood-thinner, so it is advised not to combine with blood-thinning medication. Take care to discontinue use a few weeks prior to and after surgery.[186]

ROSEHIPS

Rosehips are the fruit of a rose. Once the flower has bloomed and the petals have all fallen off, the "hip" is then plucked from the center, and that sucker has a massive quantity of medicinal values! Rosehips are anti-inflammatory,[187] antidepressant, antiviral, antiseptic, antispasmodic, and antibacterial. They're also astringent, an antioxidant, and a blood, kidney, urinary tract, and recovery tonic. Rosehips are believed to be native to Persia.

Scientific name: Rosa canina

Part used: fruit

Medicinal uses:

- Fights free radicals[188]
- Strengthens immunity[189]
- Pain-relieving
- Lowers blood pressure
- Helps gallbladder ailments[190]
- Aids urinary tract and kidney disorders
- Aids digestion distress[191]
- Helps relieve phlegm and chest congestion[192]

ROSEMARY

Rosemary is native to the Mediterranean, France, and Spain and can grow up to six feet tall! It is antispasmodic, antifungal,[193] antioxidant,[194] antidepressant, and antiseptic. It's also an expectorant, decongestant, carminative, diuretic, and both a circulatory[195] and digestive tonic.[196]

Scientific name: Rosmarinus officinalis

Part used: leaf

Medicinal uses:

- Stimulates blood flow[197]
- Supplies increased levels of oxygen to the brain
- Improves memory and concentration[198]
- Eases anxiety, tension, and depression
- Protects cells against free radical damage[199]
- Enhances nutrient absorption
- Stimulates hair growth[200]
- Resists infections
- Prevents waste accumulation in the body
- Eases inflammation[201]
- Neutralizes food-borne pathogens[202]
- Fights bronchial infections and improves breathing[203]

SAGE

Sage is a plant with beautiful, flat, soft leaves—it's unmistakable. It's anti-inflammatory,[204] antibacterial,[205] antispasmodic, antiseptic, antiaging, antibiotic, astringent, and carminative. The broad-leaf herb is also a sedative, cooling, disinfectant, and a circulatory stimulant. Sage is native to the Mediterranean.

Scientific name: Salvia officinalis

Part used: leaf

Medicinal uses:

- Strengthens the heart
- Fights infections
- Lowers blood sugar[206]
- Prevents premature aging
- Fights free radicals[207]
- Soothes the digestive tract[208]
- Lends vitality
- Eases menstrual irregularities[209]

Caution: Nursing mothers should be aware that sage can significantly decrease milk production, which can be helpful if weaning or are over-producing milk. If decreased milk production is *not* desired, then it's recommended to avoid sage.[210]

SLIPPERY ELM

Slippery elm is native to Canada and the United States and is a huge tree that grows to sixty feet tall (like a weeping willow)! It's demulcent, emollient, and detoxifying, as well as a health tonic and laxative. This herb has had serious success with treating ulcerative colitis and Crohn's disease.[211]

Scientific name: Ulmus rubra

Part used: bark

Medicinal uses:

- Soothes throat and gut inflammation[212]
- Slows diarrhea[213]
- Fights acidity[214]
- Regulates bowels[215]
- Restorative treatment for enflamed mucous membranes[216]

Caution: Like marshmallow, slippery elm works by coating the stomach lining, which can slow or hinder absorption of other medications.[217]

Spearmint

Spearmint is my favorite herb to eat raw. I grow it at home, and every time I'm in my garden, I pluck off a few leaves and chew them as I work—they are *delicious*. It's a great blending herb and is usually a child's favorite, too (which explains things about me). Spearmint is native to North America, South America, and Africa.

Scientific name: Mentha spicata

Part used: leaf, flower

Medicinal uses:

- Relieves nausea
- Calms hyperactivity
- Lessens anxiety
- Energizes and stimulates

Fun Fact

Peppermint and almost all other mint species are the children of spearmint: spearmint is the ultimate minty predecessor—the Grandfather of all Mintkind!

St. John's Wort

This herb is anti-inflammatory,[218] antiviral, antifungal, antibacterial, astringent, analgesic, and a powerful nerve tonic.[219] It's also a sedative and antidepressant. St. John's wort is native to Britain, Europe, and Asia.

Scientific name: Hypericum perforatum

Part used: flower, leaf

Medicinal uses:

- Restores and refreshes the nervous system[220]
- Decreases irritability, depression, and anxiety[221]
- Aids in the treatment of insomnia[222]
- Stabilizes mood and emotions
- Increases immunity

Caution: Don't use St. John's wort in combination with prescription antidepressants. It also increases skin sensitivity (especially to sunlight) and shouldn't be used if being treated with radiation therapy. Also, anyone pregnant or breastfeeding should consult with an herbalist or other healthcare practitioner before ingesting St. John's wort.[223]

Thyme

I think thyme is one of the prettiest herbs, and its medicinal values seem to be endless. It's antibacterial, antiviral, *very* antifungal,[224] antispasmodic, antimicrobial, and antibiotic. It's also incredibly aromatic, astringent, carminative, and diaphoretic. Thyme is an expectorant, a decongestant, an emmenagogue, and a tonic. Is there anything thyme isn't good for?! It's native to Europe.

Scientific name: Thymus vulgaris

Part used: leaf, flower

Medicinal uses:

- Aids in killing and expelling ringworm[225]
- Treats thrush in the mouth[226]
- Fights infections, growths, and fungal allergies[227]
- Clears sinuses
- Cleansing to the kidneys and urinary tract[228]
- Opens bronchial passageways; assists in cleansing the respiratory tract[229]

Turmeric

(Curcuma longa)

Turmeric is an ancient herb that has been used for centuries in Ayurveda, traditional Indian medicine, and been shown to have countless health benefits, such as being anticancer, anti-inflammatory, and analgesic.[230] However, much like eucalyptus (but for entirely different reasons), it isn't destined for tea.

To reap the rewards of turmeric, it must be combined with fat, not water. This explains why in traditional Indian cooking, the spice is often mixed with milk, cream, and/or butter.

Another reason for not drinking turmeric tea may be the certain discoloring of your teeth, lips, and possibly hands—the spice stains a deep yellow and takes a couple of days to go away. For this reason, it makes an excellent natural food coloring.

VALERIAN

Valerian is best known for its anti-inflammatory and analgesic properties. It's also fantastic in a blend for high blood pressure. Valerian is native to Asia and Europe.

Scientific name: Valeriana officinalis

Part used: root

Medicinal uses:

- Aids in the treatment of high blood pressure
- Muscle relaxing
- Aids in the treatment of insomnia
- Pain-relieving
- General heart tonic

Caution: Use moderately (not excessively) in a two-week on/two-week off rotation.[231]

WILD YAM

Wild yam is best known for its antispasmodic properties, which can assist in PMS. It also contains phytoestrogens, and although no clinic studies have proven its efficacy of late, many herbalists insist it's an essential herb for aiding women with menopause symptoms—especially hot flashes.[232] The medicinal variety is native to Mexico.

Scientific name: Dioscorea villosa

Part used: root

Medicinal uses:

- ❧ Treats menopause symptoms
- ❧ Prevents osteoporosis
- ❧ Good for heart health[233]
- ❧ Beneficial for arthritis[234] and irritable bowel syndrome (IBS)[235]

Yarrow

Yarrow is anti-inflammatory,[236] antiseptic, antispasmodic, anticancer,[237] astringent, diuretic, and diaphoretic. It's also a digestive tonic, vulnerary, and hypotensive.[238] Yarrow is native to temperate regions of Asia, Europe, and North America.

Scientific name: Achillea millefolium

Part used: leaf, flower

Medicinal uses:

- Treats digestive disorders and liver deficiencies[239]
- Relieves anxiety[240]
- Reduces inflammation[241]
- Kills infection[242]
- Breaks fever[243]
- Regulates menstrual cycles[244]
- Tones liver
- Kills parasites[245]
- Repairs damaged tissues[246]
- Prevents hair loss and baldness

Caution: Do not use if pregnant: yarrow stimulates uterine contractions.[247] It may also stimulate allergy symptoms, such as a rash and/or itchy eyes. If you experience these types of symptoms, discontinue use.[248]

YERBA MATE

Yerba Mate is native to South America, and the official drink of Argentina. Because of its energizing properties, the tea makes an excellent substitute for coffee! It is an energy, spine, and nerve tonic, and a stimulant, diuretic, laxative, and astringent.[249] It's also a rejuvenator, aperient, and purgative.[250] There are many health nuts that *swear* by the amazing yerba mate.

Scientific name: Ilex paraguariensis

Part used: leaf

Medicinal uses:

- Improves concentration and memory
- Reduces and delays lactic acid build-up[251]
- Improves motor response
- Boosts metabolism
- Fights fatigue[252]
- Combats obesity[253]
- Stimulates adrenal glands and adrenal cortex[254]

Part Three: 50 Teas for 50 Common Ailments

TEA MAKES EVERYTHING BETTER

The third portion of this book is the longest, and it's divided into three sections: Acute, Chronic, and Random + Preventative. Under each section is an alphabetical list of common disorders, medicinal plants that can help them, and an accompanying herbal tea recipe. As always, please be sure to consult an herbalist if you're unsure about blending herbs you've never tried before, or try simples in small amounts before blends. Don't drink any medicinal tea if you are currently pregnant, breastfeeding, or taking prescription medication without consulting an herbalist or another medical professional.

Although I have listed any well-documented cautions I have come across in relation to each and every herb featured, there is always the possibility of an unfavorable effect if an herb is new to you. As previously stated, everyone is different, and each and every single one of us reacts in our own way to anything we put in our bodies. Just as we can easily become aware of the effects that certain foodstuffs have on our bodies (such as dairy or sugar), we should also be alert and observant when trying new herbs.

Remember that the herbs listed in the tea recipes should be dried and from the proper part of the plant (root, stem, leaf, flower, fruit, and/or seed). Also, feel free to add a flavor enhancer if you see fit. Honey, lemon, and cinnamon are my favorite game-changers, but add whatever makes you feel good.

Are you ready to take a leap into the world of medicinal tea? Let's go!

Tea Tips to Remember:

- ❧ Follow proper storing instructions.
- ❧ Steep for 10–15 minutes, depending on desired potency and taste preference.
- ❧ Steep covered, so that the herb can fully immerse with the water.
- ❧ Use hot water, preferably filtered and boiled.
- ❧ Be aware of any possible interactions between herbs by steeping simples first and reading about the cautions and interactions associated with each herb.

ACUTE

When treating oneself with herbal tea for an acute health issue, the general rule is to administer in small, frequent doses. Therefore, each of the recipes below should be administered in half-cup portions, 4–6 times per day, for a total of 2–3 servings daily.

COLD AND FLU

Many of us are aware of at least a couple of common herbs for cold and flu. Often, over-the-counter medications for cold and flu will advertise a natural ingredient on the packaging, such as "made with echinacea!" or "with the healing power of ginseng!" But why buy meds that may insert only a tiny bit of herbal extract when you can brew the real deal at home?

When it comes to cold and flu, the variety of symptoms are bountiful: aches, pain, chills, fever, headaches, lethargy, reduced appetite, and more. The following plants are here for you—and make much safer, healthy, effective, and convenient aids. Also, who doesn't want tea when they're sick? Colds and tea go together like peanut butter and jelly. It's all about *comfort*, and the following herbs each provide unique ways to accomplish this.

Echinacea appears to be the gold standard, with research concluding that it can "shorten the duration and severity of colds and other upper respiratory infections when given as soon as symptoms become evident."[255] Tea with echinacea can be helpful if used preventatively. However, if cold symptoms have already set in, then the tincture (which is much stronger) is recommended instead.

Chamomile is soothing and calming[256] while cinnamon warms you up when you experience chills; it's also great for an upset stomach. Marshmallow coats the throat and stomach lining, helping to relieve soreness and tenderness in those areas while also performing anti-inflammatory magic;[257] ginger provides relief of nausea.[258]

While lemon and thyme both help to cut through mucous and provide an antibacterial role in aiding throat irritations,[259] thyme also has the added benefit of being a natural expectorant.[260] Lastly, plantain[261] and ginseng[262] are used to relieve upper respiratory tract infections, as does elder.[263]

Helpful Herbs

- Chamomile
- Cinnamon
- Echinacea
- Elder
- Ginger
- Ginseng
- Lemon
- Marshmallow
- Plantain
- Thyme

COMFORT IN A CUP TEA

Ingredients:
1 part chamomile flower
1 part ginger root
1 part lemon peel
1 part echinacea root
8 oz. hot water

Directions:
Combine dried herbs and steep in water, covered, for 10–15 minutes.
Remove herbs from water, and sip tea slowly.

Constipation

Constipation is a very common complaint: 15–25 percent of Americans suffer from it on a chronic basis at some point throughout their lives.[264] There are many herbs that relieve constipation, including the ones I've listed below. Ingesting herbal tea as a prescription for constipation works beautifully for two reasons: the herbs stimulate, coat, and/or soothe the digestive tract, making it easier to eliminate, and all of that fluid gives stool an extra push out.

Anise, dandelion, fennel, and slippery elm are all great herbs for this affliction. Slippery elm works by coating the lining of the intestine, thereby making bowel movements easier and more productive.[265] Fennel[266] and anise[267] stimulate bowel movements, and dandelion is a natural, mild laxative.[268]

You shouldn't have to drink more than 1 or 2 servings of the tea recipe below to experience its effects.

Helpful Herbs

- Anise
- Dandelion
- Fennel
- Slippery elm

Smooth Move Tea

Ingredients:
1 part anise seed
2 parts dandelion root
8 oz. hot water

Directions:
Combine dried herbs and steep in water, covered, for 10–15 minutes.
Remove herbs from water, and sip tea slowly.

COUGH

Coughing is a natural way for your body to rid the lungs of foreign substances, such as phlegm, mucous, and bacteria. Typically, coughing helps your body, but when sleep is disrupted or harsh, persistent coughing tears the bronchial tubes leading to infection, cough can (and should) be stifled.

Although there are many over-the-counter cough medications available to us today, the best are homemade herbal teas. The plants listed below have all been proven to treat and suppress cough, and/or soothe the throat, minimizing associated pain.[269]

Helpful Herbs

- Anise
- Peppermint
- Slippery elm
- Thyme
- White horehound

Soothing Silencer Tea

Ingredients:
1 part thyme leaf
2 parts white horehound leaf
8 oz. hot water

Directions:
Combine dried herbs and steep in water, covered, for 10–15 minutes.
Remove herbs from water, and sip tea slowly.

DIARRHEA

Diarrhea is a major bummer, and when it happens to you, you'll do anything to make it stop. The following herbs work wonders for stopping diarrhea swiftly without the side effect of turning what's left in your bowels into cement.

Bilberry's astringent value helps to tighten and constrict tissue while easing intestinal spasms and reducing bowel inflammation.[270] Similarly, raspberry leaf helps to control diarrhea by restricting the flow of fluids into the intestines, thereby solidifying the stool.[271]

Tea for diarrhea works best if taken cold, as warm liquid may induce further loose stool before the remedy has the chance to work.

Helpful Herbs

- Bilberry
- Raspberry leaf

The Screeching Halt Tea

Ingredients:
1 part raspberry leaf
1 part bilberry fruit
8 oz. hot water

Directions:
Combine dried herbs and steep in water, covered, for 10–15 minutes.
Remove herbs from water, and pour tea over ice. Sip slowly.

DIGESTIVE DISTRESS (GENERAL)

The term "digestive distress" can allude to anything from nausea to indigestion and everything in between, but each of the following herbs offer symptomatic relief. Anise will ward of nausea[272] while fennel has been found to relieve colic and reduce intestinal spasms.[273]

One of the most popular herbs for easing digestive issues is peppermint, which has been shown to greatly reduce nausea, symptoms of irritable bowel syndrome (IBS), indigestion, and intestinal spasms.[274]

Countless research studies conclude that slippery elm is extremely beneficial in relieving symptoms related to ulcerative colitis and Crohn's disease, which are serious autoimmune digestive disorders,[275] while yarrow "increases saliva and stomach acid, helping to improve digestion."[276] Fennel has also been found to promote digestive-enhancing activities.[277]

Helpful Herbs

- Anise
- Chamomile
- Fennel
- Lemon balm
- Peppermint
- Slippery elm
- Yarrow

Tummy Tamer Tea

Ingredients:
1 part fennel seed
1 part yarrow leaf and flower
2 parts peppermint leaf
8 oz. hot water

Directions:
Combine dried herbs and steep in water, covered, for 10–15 minutes.
Remove herbs from water, and sip tea slowly.

Fatigue

The following herbs are well known for their wakeful values. Ginseng has the ability to reduce mental fatigue, and improve cognitive performance and memory speed[278] while yerba mate and peppermint have both been shown to "increase mental focus and clarity."[279] Rosemary can also be stimulating for the brain.

Helpful Herbs

- Ginseng
- Peppermint
- Rosemary
- Yerba mate

Wakeful Tea

Ingredients:
1 part rosemary leaf
1 part ginseng root
8 oz. hot water

Directions:
Combine dried herbs and steep in water, covered, for 10–15 minutes.
Remove herbs from water, and sip tea slowly.

FEVER

The following herbs can be made into a tea and sipped to lower body temperature and break a fever. Lemon is popularly prescribed for fever reduction and is probably the most effective.[280] Feverfew[281] (it's in the name!) and yarrow[282] have both been traditionally used to treat fevers, as well as a host of other inflammatory conditions.

Helpful Herbs

- Feverfew
- Lemon peel
- Yarrow

Cooling Tea

Ingredients:
1 part yarrow leaf and flower
2 parts lemon peel
8 oz. hot water

Directions:
Combine dried herbs and steep in water, covered, for 10–15 minutes.
Remove herbs from water, and sip tea slowly.
*Feel free to sweeten with honey if tea is too tart.

HANGOVER

Hangovers happen, right? And when they do, you don't want to regret the previous night; you want to deal with it quickly and move on. "Hangover" is a broad term used to describe lack of sleep, nausea, and typically low blood sugar levels caused by excessive alcohol consumption, and the herbs below will help combat these symptoms.

Peppermint helps to relieve nausea and clear the head, while alleviating headaches and cooling inflamed tissue.[283] Milk thistle has been shown to have an anti-inflammatory and antioxidant effect on the liver and can assist in further detox.[284] Ginkgo produces a stimulating effect and can help increase cognitive function. Plantain is effective in removing toxins from the blood.[285]

Helpful Herbs

- Ginkgo
- Milk thistle
- Peppermint
- Plantain

Get Over It! Tea

Ingredients:
1 part milk thistle seed
1 part peppermint leaf
8 oz. hot water

Directions:
Combine dried herbs and steep in water, covered, for 10–15 minutes.
Remove herbs from water, and sip tea slowly.

Hay Fever

Seasonal allergies can be *such* a literal pain for so many of us. The symptoms that we may experience (itchy, watery eyes, runny nose, headaches, and sneezing) are the result of inflammation caused by your sinuses being alerted to foreign pathogens (pollens) in the air. Sip your way to a symptom-free spring with a li'l medicinal tea.

Eyebright is known for being effective in treating ocular allergy symptoms when the tea is used to make a compress,[286] and lemon balm works by sweeping your sinuses clean of bacteria and viruses[287] and calming throat constriction.

Nettle contains histamines, which (ironically enough) have been shown to treat allergies, asthma, and hay fever,[288] and thyme helps to relieve respiratory symptoms associated with hay fever.

Helpful Herbs

- Elder
- Eyebright
- Lemon balm
- Nettle
- Thyme

Hay Fever Tea

Ingredients:
1 part lemon balm
1 part elder
2 parts nettle
8 oz. hot water

Directions:
Combine dried herbs and steep in water, covered, for 10–15 minutes.
Remove herbs from water, and sip tea slowly.

HEADACHES

Herbal treatment of headaches are very similar to that of migraines with the main difference being that migraines usually need to be treated as soon as possible to lessen the overall severity; headaches are less serious and seem to be more easily treated in general.

Feverfew,[289] lavender,[290] and peppermint[291] are the gold standards for holistic headache treatment. Rosemary is another herb that has been deemed scientifically helpful.[292]

Helpful Herbs

- ❧ Feverfew
- ❧ Lavender
- ❧ Peppermint
- ❧ Rosemary

Headache-Away Tea

Ingredients:
1 part lavender flower
1 part peppermint leaf
8 oz. hot water

Directions:
Combine dried herbs and steep in water, covered, for 10–15 minutes. Remove herbs from water, and sip tea slowly.

Heartburn

Medically termed "gastroesophogeal reflux disease" or GERD, heartburn can make eating and drinking a nightmare. Some suffer less than others, but in any case, the condition flat-out sucks. Some herbs that can assist in heartburn relief are cinnamon, licorice, marshmallow, and slippery elm. It's important to note that if your heartburn is chronic, permanent dietary changes should be implemented, and these herbs will only provide temporary relief of symptoms.

Slippery elm and marshmallow coat the stomach and throat, thereby providing a protective layer against acid or bile.[293] Cinnamon and licorice provide support for the upper digestive tract and should be taken as soon as one feels heartburn commence.[294] (They can also be used preventatively.)

Helpful Herbs

- Cinnamon
- Licorice
- Marshmallow
- Slippery elm

BURN AWAY TEA

Ingredients:
1 part licorice root
2 parts marshmallow root
8 oz. hot water

Directions:
Combine dried herbs and steep in water, covered, for 10–15 minutes.
Remove herbs from water, and sip tea slowly.
*If the hot temperature further aggravates symptoms, consider taking the tea cold by brewing for 2 minutes longer, then pouring the concoction over ice.

Hyperactivity

Hyperactivity can plague anyone, but children are especially prone. Sadly, many Western physicians seem to have no problem with whipping out a prescription pad and submitting a request for commercialized drugs.

Alternative treatments recommend that hyperactivity can be largely dealt with by way of dietary intervention and limiting one's sugar, artificial colors, preservatives, and making certain one's hearing and vision are running smoothly.

Spearmint, chamomile, lavender, and lemon balm are all plants that are widely used by herbalists to calm and relax one's nervous system and brain activity.

Helpful Herbs

- Chamomile
- Lavender
- Lemon balm
- Spearmint

Hyperactivi-Tea

Ingredients:
1 part lemon balm leaf
1 part spearmint leaf
8 oz. hot water

Directions:
Combine dried herbs and steep in water, covered, for 10–15 minutes.
Remove herbs from water, and sip tea slowly.
*This tea is completely safe for everyone, in any quantity.

Migraines

A migraine is typically described as a longer-lasting, more severe headache. Several factors can cause them, including stress and food allergies. Some environmental things can worsen them, such as bright light and noise. Those who are "prone" to migraines (it seems that you either get them or you don't) know that the key to stopping them early is to recognize the symptoms as soon as they begin and to treat immediately.

Feverfew,[295] lavender,[296] peppermint,[297] and dong quai[298] have all been shown through peer-reviewed studies to be effective in managing a migraine headache.

Helpful Herbs

- Dong quai
- Feverfew
- Lavender
- Peppermint

Tea for Migraines

Ingredients:
1 part peppermint leaf
1 part lavender flower
2 parts dong quai root and leaf
8 oz. hot water

Directions:
Combine dried herbs and steep in water, covered, for 10–15 minutes.
Remove herbs from water, and sip tea slowly.

MUSCLE TENSION

Chamomile, cramp bark, peppermint, and wild yam have all been proven to assist in relieving muscle tension.

While cramp bark is most effective at relieving tension in the abdominal and back regions,[299] peppermint is fairly beneficial throughout the entire body and also provides pain relief.[300] Wild yam is an extremely beneficial herb for treating fibromyalgia, a condition in which muscle and joint pain proliferates,[301] and valerian is a great muscle relaxant.[302] Chamomile is stress-relieving and thereby relieves muscular tension.

Helpful Herbs

- Chamomile
- Cramp bark
- Peppermint
- Valerian
- Wild yam

TEA FOR GENERAL MUSCLE RELIEF

Ingredients:
1 part chamomile flower
1 part valerian root
8 oz. hot water

Directions:
Combine dried herbs and steep in water, covered, for 10–15 minutes.
Remove herbs from water, and sip tea slowly.
*Feel free to replace the chamomile and/or valerian with herbs that are
more specific to targeted muscle groups, barring any interactions that may
be especially pertinent to you. For example, if attempting to target tight
muscles in the back, one could swap valerian for cramp bark.

NAUSEA

Whether its origin lies in travel, pregnancy, a virus, or a hangover, nausea is the *worst*. Anise,[303] ginger,[304] peppermint,[305] and spearmint are all incredible herbs for combatting an unstable stomach, and each one works swiftly.

Helpful Herbs

- Anise
- Ginger
- Peppermint
- Spearmint

Stomach Stabilizing Tea

Ingredients
1 part ginger root
2 parts peppermint leaf
8 oz. hot water

Directions:
Combine dried herbs and steep in water, covered, for 10–15 minutes. Remove herbs from water, and sip tea slowly.

PAIN

Pain is something everyone experiences; it's an unfortunate inevitability, whether in the form of a toothache, headache, backache, or other pain entirely. General pain calls for herbs that are analgesic, simply meaning that they're pain-relieving in their nature. Examples of analgesic commercial pain relievers are acetaminophen and aspirin, but herbal tea is much kinder to your body since some commercial pain medications cause abdominal pain, are addictive, or present the possibility of overdose.

Black cohosh has been used to help relieve pain associated with childbirth and arthritis as well as breast, uterine, and ovarian pain.[306] Studies have proven that chamomile has a sedative, mild analgesic, and sleepy effect on those who consume it,[307] and cramp bark is particularly useful in relieving abdominal pain.[308] Peppermint[309] and valerian[310] have both been found to relieve muscle pain as well as pain associated with breastfeeding, shingles, and headaches.

Helpful Herbs

- Black cohosh
- Chamomile
- Cramp bark
- Peppermint
- Valerian

Pain Away Tea

Ingredients:
1 part peppermint leaf
1 part cramp bark
1 part valerian root
8 oz. hot water

Directions:
Combine dried herbs and steep in water, covered, for 10–15 minutes.
Remove herbs from water, and sip tea slowly.

Respiratory

There are many herbs that have been proven successful in aiding respiratory distress, and the plants listed below are Mother Nature's hard hitters.

Asthmatic respiratory issues can be vastly improved by taking plantain[311] and rosemary[312] tea, which assists in opening tightened bronchial tubes. (See Asthma on page 124.) Peppermint, plantain, and thyme are all decongestants, but the latter two are also expectorants, meaning they help to loosen phlegm so it can be coughed up and out.

Lungwort is a total lung tonic which kills and prevents respiratory infection, as well as assists in asthmatic and bronchial issues,[313] as does eyebright.[314] White horehound[315] and mullein[316] treat asthmatic phlegm, nagging cough, wheezing, shortness of breath, and other breathing difficulties; they are both useful in treating bronchitis.

Helpful Herbs

- Eyebright
- Lungwort
- Mullein
- Peppermint
- Plantain
- Rosemary
- Thyme
- White horehound

Breathe Better Tea

Ingredients:
1 part rosemary leaf
1 part lungwort leaf
2 parts white horehound leaf
8 oz. hot water

Directions:
Combine dried herbs and steep in water, covered, for 10–15 minutes.
Remove herbs from water, and sip tea slowly.

URINARY TRACT INFECTIONS

Urinary tract infections (UTIs) are very common—especially among females. Symptoms can include redness, itchiness, abdominal pain, a burning sensation during urination, and as it progresses, fever and even nausea.

The most common plant cure for a UTI is cranberry.[317] Cranberry "juice" is often actually a cocktail full of sugar, which feeds infection. It's much more effective to steep the fruit and drink as a tea. Burdock has recently been found to facilitate "the host immune system to fight infections."[318] Other herbs that are helpful include dandelion,[319] horsetail,[320, 321] marshmallow,[322] raspberry leaf,[323] and thyme.[324]

Horsetail and dandelion help to remove bacteria in the urinary tract, and "marshmallow inhibits bacterial growth and cleanses the bladder."[325] Cranberry contains natural antibiotics and is a fabulous diuretic, so that's why it works wonders![326]

Helpful Herbs

- Burdock
- Cranberry
- Dandelion
- Horsetail
- Marshmallow
- Raspberry leaf
- Thyme

U Tea I

Ingredients
1 part cranberry fruit
2 parts horsetail leaf
8 oz. hot water

Directions
Combine dried herbs and steep in water, covered, for 10–15 minutes.
Remove herbs from water, and sip tea slowly.

WORMS

Intestinal worms are (unfortunately) pretty common. It's not unusual for young children to contract pinworms due to fecal contamination when potty training and then unknowingly pass them on to the entire family. Also, many of us pick them up while visiting foreign countries or eating various foods that have been previously contaminated.

Feverfew,[327] hops,[328] white horehound,[329] and thyme[330] have been proven effective in killing and/or expelling a variety of worm species. Teas made from these herbs are kinder to your digestive tract, effective, and don't contain the added harmful preparation of commercial medications. Remember that when one is being treated for worms, the entire family should be treated, and sheets, towels, and clothing should be rotated and cleaned daily for up to two weeks.

Helpful Herbs

- Feverfew (worms, in general)
- Hops (worms, in general)
- Thyme (ringworm)
- White horehound (worms, in general)

WORM-AWAY TEA

Ingredients:
1 part hops flower
2 parts white horehound leaf
8 oz. hot water

Directions:
Combine dried herbs and steep in water, covered, for 10–15 minutes.
Remove herbs from water, and sip tea slowly.
*Consume 4 servings of this tea per day for two weeks.

Yeast Infections

The most common types of yeast infections are vaginal infections and thrush, the latter of which is an oral yeast infection that infants commonly contract. All yeast infections are due to an overgrowth of Candida albicans and are typically caused by overuse of antibiotics, pregnancy, and other health conditions, such as a weakened immune system and diabetes.[331]

Yeast infections are fungal and therefore need to be treated with antifungal herbs. One of the strongest of these is thyme,[332] which has an "anticandidal agent."[333] Cinnamon[334] and rosemary are both powerfully anti-fungal[335] and have the ability to kill yeast cells. Adding sage[336] to one's diet can also be helpful.

Helpful Herbs

- Cinnamon
- Rosemary
- Sage
- Thyme

Yeast-Be-Gone Tea

Ingredients:
1 part rosemary leaf
1 part thyme leaf
8 oz. hot water

Directions:
Combine dried herbs and steep in water, covered, for 10–15 minutes.
Remove herbs from water, and sip tea slowly.

CHRONIC

When treating for a chronic health issue, it's recommended to consume large doses over a long duration of time—with consistency being the key. Therefore, when using one of the tea recipes in this section, the dosage is 1 serving, every 5 hours while awake, for a total of 3 servings of tea per day.

Allergies

The herbs listed below have been found medicinally helpful in improving allergy symptoms and providing respiratory relief. Although the term "allergies" is often used loosely to refer to *seasonal* allergies, this section is different than the one on hay fever because, while hay fever presents annoying symptoms, the results aren't as serious as outright allergy symptoms can be.

I want to stress that if anyone is experiencing throat closure or anaphylactic signs, they (or someone else who might be present) should not hesitate to use prescribed inhalers and/or call paramedics *immediately*.

Eyebright is helpful in easing ocular allergy symptoms when the tea is used to make an eye compress[337] while lemon balm cleans the sinuses and has a calming effect on the nervous system.[338] Feverfew inhibits histamine release which helps to minimize symptoms. [339]

Helpful Herbs

- Eyebright
- Feverfew
- Lemon balm

Tea for Allergy

Ingredients:
1 part feverfew leaf
1 part lemon balm leaf
8 oz. hot water

Directions:
Combine dried herbs and steep in water, covered, for 10–15 minutes.
Remove herbs from water, and sip tea slowly.
*For eye relief: combine 1 tablespoon eyebright stem, leaf, and flower with
10 ounces of hot water, and let steep for 20–30 minutes. Remove herbs,
and thoroughly soak a clean cloth in tea. Let cloth cool, then place over
eyes.

ANEMIA

Anemia is a condition in which one possesses lower than ideal iron stores. Most of Canada and the United States can be considered anemic, mostly due to the popular acceptance of the "Western diet"—that is, a diet that does not include enough iron-rich foods.

Symptoms of anemia are chronic fatigue, listlessness, pale skin, dizziness, shortness of breath, and weakness.[340] Hawthorn,[341] nettle,[342] and dandelion, whose "leaves have a high iron content and enhance the absorption of iron from other sources,"[343] are three herbs that can help provide iron and increase iron absorption greatly if taken on a regular basis.

Helpful Herbs

- Dandelion
- Hawthorn
- Nettle

Iron-Up Tea

Ingredients:
1 part dandelion leaf
1 part nettle leaf
8 oz. hot water

Directions:
Combine dried herbs and steep in water, covered, for 10–15 minutes.
Remove herbs from water, and sip tea slowly.

ANXIETY

The Mayo Clinic defines anxiety as "intense, excessive and persistent worry and fear about everyday situations."[344] The following herbs each help in their own ways to combat this disorder naturally, and since prescription medications for anxiety have so many side effects, they are well worth a try.

Chamomile,[345] lemon balm,[346] and hops[347] have all been proven to relieve tension and anxiety, and a 2009 study concluded that lavender and rosemary are both successful herbs in reducing test anxiety.[348] Similarly, St. John's wort is often prescribed by herbalists and medical doctors alike for its success in treating mild anxiety,[349] and so is yarrow.[350]

Helpful Herbs

- ᕯ Chamomile
- ᕯ Hops
- ᕯ Lavender
- ᕯ Lemon balm
- ᕯ Rosemary
- ᕯ St. John's wort
- ᕯ Yarrow

Anti-AnxieTea

Ingredients:
1 part chamomile flower
1 part lemon balm leaf
2 parts St. John's wort flower
8 oz. hot water

Directions:
Combine dried herbs and steep in water, covered, for 10–15 minutes. Remove herbs from water, and sip tea slowly.

ARTHRITIS

Arthritis is essentially chronic inflammation present in one or more joints. The goal of medicinal tea should be to reduce inflammation as well as manage the pain associated with the condition.

Chamomile has been proven moderately successful in reducing swelling and inflammation,[351] as has feverfew.[352] A 2013 study found both ginger and cinnamon to be extremely beneficial in reducing muscle and joint inflammation and pain among female athletes,[353] and rosehips,[354] nettle,[355] and wild yam[356] are particularly helpful in reducing joint pain and other arthritic symptoms as well.

Helpful Herbs

- Chamomile
- Cinnamon
- Feverfew
- Ginger
- Nettle
- Rosehips
- Wild yam

TEA FOR JOINT PAIN

Ingredients:
1 part chamomile flower
1 part rosehips flower
2 parts wild yam root
8 oz. hot water

Directions:
Combine dried herbs and steep in water, covered, for 10–15 minutes.
Remove herbs from water, and sip tea slowly.

ASTHMA

Symptoms of asthma can be triggered by a variety of offenders. For most, triggers include weather, exercise, mood and emotion, and pet dander. These circumstances create respiratory problems that range from mild to severe, and many who are diagnosed carry prescribed steroids in the form of bronchial inhalers to help ease symptoms.

Thyme soothes muscle constriction and prevents and alleviates asthma symptoms by relieving muscle tightness in the bronchi,[357] and nettle has been proven extremely effective in treating symptoms of asthma.[358] A recent study conducted by the Department of Respiratory Disease in China concluded that ginkgo "could significantly decrease the infiltration of inflammatory cells . . . in the asthmatic airway and relieve the airway inflammation."[359]

Lemon balm calms smooth muscle spasms and limits throat constriction[360] while feverfew and lungwort have both been shown to help relieve symptoms of asthma.[361]

Helpful Herbs

- Feverfew
- Ginkgo
- Lemon balm
- Lungwort
- Nettle
- Thyme

Breathe Easy Tea

Ingredients:
1 part thyme leaf
1 part nettle leaf
2 parts lungwort leaf
8 oz. hot water

Directions:
Combine dried herbs and steep in water, covered, for 10–15 minutes.
Remove herbs from water, and sip tea slowly.

BLOOD PRESSURE

Ginger, green tea, hawthorn, valerian, and yarrow can all be used to help lower high blood pressure, which is also termed "hypertension."

Ginger helps by blocking the voltage-dependent calcium channels, but those who take medication for this ailment should not use ginger in conjunction with it.[362] In traditional Chinese medicine, green tea,[363] hawthorn, and valerian have been recognized for hundreds of years for their blood pressure-lowering benefits,[364] and yarrow has been proven to tone the blood, improve circulation, and aid in hypertension reduction.[365]

Helpful Herbs

- Ginger
- Green Tea
- Hawthorn
- Valerian
- Yarrow

Turn Down the Pressure Cooker! Tea

Ingredients:
1 part valerian root
1 part hawthorn leaf, fruit, or flower
1 part green tea leaf
8 oz. hot water

Directions:
Combine herbs and steep in water, covered, for 10–15 minutes.
Remove herbs from water, and sip tea slowly.

Blood Sugar

If you're looking for ways to lower your blood sugar, the following herbs will come to your rescue. Both ginseng and green tea are well known to decrease blood sugar levels,[366] and burdock has been used for many years in the treatment of diabetes.[367] Sage tea has "shown to be as effective as metformin, which is an oral anti-diabetic drug used for the treatment of type-2 diabetes,"[368] and marshmallow root can also help, though it's not as measurable as the others.[369]

Helpful Herbs

- Burdock
- Ginseng
- Green Tea
- Marshmallow
- Sage

Not-So-Sweet Tea

Ingredients:
1 part sage leaf
2 parts burdock root
8 oz. hot water

Directions:
Combine dried herbs and steep in water, covered, for 10–15 minutes.
Remove herbs from water, and sip tea slowly.
*Feel free to sweeten with honey.

CHOLESTEROL

Many of the cholesterol-lowering commercial drugs on the market today (statins) come with considerable side effects.[370] The herbs listed below can help lower cholesterol naturally and are generally deemed a safer alternative in the world of holistic medicine. As with blood pressure, ginger, ginseng, and green tea are go-to herbs for this job.

Population-based clinical studies have found that when comparing men who drink green tea on a regular basis to those who don't, the green tea drinkers had significantly lower cholesterol levels.[371] Ginger has also been deemed helpful,[372] as has ginseng.[373]

Helpful Herbs

- Ginger
- Ginseng
- Green Tea

Cholesterol-Lowering Tea

Ingredients:
1 part ginger root
2 parts green tea leaf
8 oz. hot water

Directions:
Combine dried herbs and steep in water, covered, for 10–15 minutes.
Remove herbs from water, and sip tea slowly.

DEPRESSION

There is a huge difference between mild and severe cases of depression, and severe depression should always be treated clinically with the help of a physician. Mild forms of depression are easier to treat with herbal medicine.

Besides making sure you are getting enough sunshine (plenty of vitamin D), regular exercise, and are consuming a good diet, there are also a handful of herbs that can aid and combat depression successfully—the most notable being St. John's wort.[374] Others include ginseng, hawthorn, lavender, lemon balm, and milk thistle.

Recent studies have found "significant effects of ginseng supplements on wellbeing and depression, compared with placebo."[375] Lavender[376] and lemon balm[377] are both able to create feelings of calmness and relaxation in those who consume it, and they can be used to treat mild depression.

Finally, Rosemary Gladstar, the "godmother of modern herbalism," states that hawthorn is one of her "favorite remedies for grief and deep sadness."[378]

Helpful Herbs

- Ginseng
- Hawthorn
- Lavender
- Lemon balm
- St. John's wort

Anti-Depressant Tea

Ingredients:
1 part lemon balm leaf
1 part hawthorn leaf, flower, or berry
2 parts St. John's wort flower and leaf
8 oz. hot water

Directions:
Combine dried herbs and steep in water, covered, for 10–15 minutes.
Remove herbs from water, and sip tea slowly.
*Feel free to sweeten with honey.

DIVERTICULITIS

Diverticulitis is characterized by small pouches or pockets that form on the inside of the intestinal tract. When these pouches become filled with food debris and inflamed, infection and abscess can occur, which results in inflammation and triggers painful flare-ups worthy of lengthy hospital visits and intravenous (IV) antibiotics.

Fennel and lemon balm help to soothe stomach inflammation and provide assistance to the mucus membranes in the digestive tract,[379] and slippery elm "protects irritated tissues and promotes healing."[380] Fenugreek[381] is anti-inflammatory, licorice[382] can help soothe the gut, and ginkgo is known for its circulatory-enhancing effects.[383]

The University of Maryland Medical Center also reports that marshmallow and chamomile "may help reduce inflammation and spasms in your gastrointestinal tract and soothe mucus membranes by forming a protective coating over your inflamed areas."[384]

Helpful Herbs

- Chamomile
- Fennel
- Fenugreek
- Ginkgo
- Lemon balm
- Licorice
- Marshmallow
- Slippery elm

Tea for Diverticular Disease

Ingredients:
1 part fennel seed
1 part slippery elm bark
8 oz. hot water

Directions:
Combine dried herbs and steep in water, covered, for 10–15 minutes.
Remove herbs from water, and sip tea slowly.

Inflammation

Inflammation can occur anywhere in the body; it's our amazing body's way of protecting itself against what it deems to be foreign or dangerous. Where there's inflammation, there's a problem, and it's been hypothesized to be the root cause of all chronic disease.

Bottom line? Get rid of your inflammation. Here's how:

Sage can be used to treat "inflammation of the throat, tonsils, mucus membranes and mouth."[385] Rosehips[386] and nettle[387] are both known for aiding joint and muscle inflammation (disorders such as arthritis and rheumatism), and rosemary[388] and licorice[389] are fantastic general anti-inflammatories. Finally, bilberry reduces bowel inflammation.[390]

Helpful Herbs

- Bilberry
- Licorice
- Nettle
- Rosehips
- Rosemary
- Sage

Anti-Inflammatory Tea

Ingredients:
1 part rosehips
1 part nettle leaf
8 oz. hot water

Directions:
Combine dried herbs and steep in water, covered, for 10–15 minutes.
Remove herbs from water, and sip tea slowly.

Inflammatory Bowel Disease

This disorder encompasses ulcerative colitis and Crohn's disease; both of which are auto-immune and can be absolutely awful to live with. Inflammation reduction is imperative because it can and does get worse. Often, those who are unable to alleviate symptoms will eventually have to undergo a bowel resection. This disease has also shown a strong correlation with colorectal cancer.[391]

Slippery elm is one of the most successful herbs in treating IBD. It works by creating a mucous-like substance (once mixed with water) that works to coat inflamed tissue, especially the digestive tract.[392] Bilberry is another fabulous herb for reducing bowel inflammation, and it also works to combat intestinal spasms and diarrhea, which are common symptoms of IBD.[393]

A 2012 study proved rosehips to be specifically successful in treating IBD[394] while marshmallow is a fantastic medicinal herb for treating inflamed tissue.[395] Antimicrobials such as hops and plantain are also key to IBD management because they foster friendly gut environments that allow proper nutrient absorption. Licorice is also a great herb that falls under the IBD category because it has a soothing effect on the intestinal wall.[396]

Helpful Herbs

- Bilberry
- Hops
- Licorice
- Marshmallow
- Plantain
- Rosehips
- Slippery elm

Happy Healthy Gut Tea

Ingredients:
1 part plantain leaf and seed
1 part licorice root
2 parts slippery elm bark
8 oz. hot water

Directions:
Combine dried herbs and steep in water, covered, for 10–15 minutes.
Remove herbs from water, and sip tea slowly.

INSOMNIA

Not being able to fall or stay asleep is the *worst*. There can be many causes of insomnia, the more common ones being adrenal fatigue, stress, lifestyle choices (food and alcohol), and prescription medication. If you think your issue might be that last one, please consult an herbalist before introducing any herbs in order to avoid any unfavorable interactions with commercial medications.

Chamomile is an excellent herb for calming and relaxing the nervous system. It can be "used as a mild sedative to calm nerves and reduce anxiety, to treat hysteria, nightmares, insomnia and other sleep problems."[397] Hops and valerian are other great herbs for treating restlessness, tension, anxiety, sleep disorders, and insomnia.[398] Lemon balm works to promote sleep,[399] and licorice is an adrenal toner, which combats stress and aids against restlessness.[400]

Helpful Herbs

- Chamomile
- Hops
- Lemon balm
- Licorice
- Valerian

Sleep Tight Tea

Ingredients:
1 part lemon balm leaf
1 part chamomile flower
2 parts hops flower
8 oz. hot water

Directions:
Combine dried herbs and steep in water, covered, for 10–15 minutes.
Remove herbs from water, and sip tea slowly.

Irritable Bowel Syndrome

The symptoms of IBS can be treated with the following herbs: bilberry[401] (for intestinal spasms, inflammation, and diarrhea), chamomile (to soothe and calm the digestive tract), cramp bark[402] (for abdominal and back pain relief, as well as for its antispasmodic values), licorice[403] (to reduce inflammation in the gut), and wild yam[404] (for general treatment of IBS symptoms).

Other herbs that are great for IBS include ginger, lemon balm, and fennel for their ability to reduce stomach inflammation and soothe mucus membranes[405] and slippery elm[406] to soothe and coat the intestinal lining, thereby reducing pain and irritation. Peppermint has also been shown to be extremely beneficial in reducing symptoms of IBS.[407]

Helpful Herbs

- Bilberry
- Chamomile
- Cramp bark
- Fennel
- Ginger
- Lemon balm
- Licorice
- Peppermint
- Slippery elm
- Wild yam

Tummy Tamer Tea

Ingredients:
1 part lemon balm leaf
1 part ginger root
2 parts cramp bark
8 oz. hot water

Directions:
Combine dried herbs and steep in water, covered, for 10–15 minutes.
Remove herbs from water, and sip tea slowly.

MENOPAUSE

There are many herbs that can help relieve menopause symptoms, which approximately 70 percent of women experience. The most common symptoms include hot flashes, mood swings, vaginal dryness, insomnia, and restlessness.

Black cohosh improves symptoms of menopause and premenstrual syndrome due to chemicals in the plant that mimic the effects of estrogen; it has consistently been used medically in several European counties for over fifty years.[408] Sage and red clover are wonder-herbs which combat hot flashes and night sweats while balancing hormones.[409] Wild yam is a "remedy for menstrual discomfort and menopausal symptoms, and has also been suggested as an alternative to hormone replacement therapy (HRT)."[410]

Helpful Herbs

- Black cohosh
- Red clover
- Sage
- Wild yam

Hot Tea for Hot Flashes

Ingredients:
1 part black cohosh root
1 part red clover flower
8 oz. hot water

Directions:
Combine dried herbs and steep in water, covered, for 10–15 minutes.
Remove herbs from water, and sip tea slowly.
*Feel free to sweeten with honey.
*Enjoy up to two cups of this tea per day, but first consult with an herbalist
if you know your hormones are significantly imbalanced.

Premenstrual Syndrome

Premenstrual syndrome (PMS) is a term used to describe what the majority of women experience around the time of their periods. Symptoms include pain, bloating, abdominal cramping, swelling, gas, irritableness, and general hormonal imbalance.

Like menopause, black cohosh aids PMS because it mimics estrogen, which regulates hormones if there is an estrogen deficiency.[411] Chamomile is great for reducing swelling and inflammation,[412] and cramp bark—you guessed it—eases abdominal cramps.[413]

Nettle works to reduce bloating and water retention,[414] and yarrow regulates menstruation, eases pain, and reduces inflammation.[415] Dong quai works to stabilize hormones and eases stomach cramps and bloating.[416] Dandelion leaf helps to reduce bloating and stabilize mood swings.[417]

Helpful Herbs

- Black cohosh
- Chamomile
- Cramp bark
- Dandelion
- Dong quai
- Nettle
- Yarrow

PMS Tea

Ingredients:
1 part nettle leaf
1 part dandelion leaf
2 parts dong quai root and/or leaf
8 oz. hot water

Directions:
Combine dried herbs and steep in water, covered, for 10–15 minutes. Remove herbs from water, and sip tea slowly.

STRESS

Stress is something we all have to live with and can be both good and bad. Minimal to moderate amounts of stress can be motivating and provoking, which can lead to better work outcomes and general life satisfaction. The problem lies with chronic stress, which can interfere with sleep and change our internal body composition.

Ginseng has been deemed helpful in fighting symptoms of chronic (long-lasting) stress[418] while ginkgo is better at managing acute (sudden-onset) stress.[419] One very common symptom of stress, chronic fatigue, has been shown to be relieved with licorice root,[420] and chamomile[421] and peppermint are both herbs that have been shown to be soothing and calming on the nervous and digestive systems.

Helpful Herbs

- Chamomile
- Ginkgo
- Ginseng
- Licorice
- Peppermint

DE-STRESS TEA

Ingredients:
1 part chamomile flower
1 part licorice root
2 parts ginkgo leaf
8 oz. hot water

Directions:
Combine dried herbs and steep in water, covered, for 10–15 minutes. Remove herbs from water, and sip tea slowly.

RANDOM + PREVENTATIVE

When consuming medicinal tea preventatively, it's recommended to drink one to two servings per day. Just be aware of any herbs that are not recommended for long-term use, and if they aren't, be sure to drink them on a rotating schedule (one week on, one week off).

ADRENAL HEALTH

Your adrenal glands are your stress and hormone regulators. Although you can't see or feel them, they play an incredibly important role in maintaining health and wellness throughout your body.[422]

There are many symptoms of adrenal weakness and/or exhaustion that are very easy to overlook. These include unexpected weight gain, lethargy, and hair loss.[423] Adrenals can become fatigued by: chronic stress, hormone disruptions (such as when women go through menopause), and even tumor growth. Poor diet, insufficient sleep, and substance abuse can also contribute to overworked adrenals.[424]

Ginseng, ginkgo, and licorice[425] are all well-known herbs that can assist in adrenal strengthening and recovery.[426] Yerba mate is energizing, rejuvenating, and assists in weight loss[427] while rosehips are extremely anti-inflammatory.[428]

Helpful Herbs

- Ginkgo
- Ginseng
- Licorice
- Rosehips
- Yerba mate

A Drink for Adrenals

Ingredients:
1 part licorice root
1 part ginkgo leaf
8 oz. hot water

Directions:
Combine dried herbs and steep in water, covered, for 10–15 minutes. Remove herbs from water, and sip tea slowly.

ATHLETIC PERFORMANCE AND RECOVERY

Many athletes are on the continuous search for anything that will help them gain an edge over their competition. Although food and over-the-counter preparations may help, they're not as pure and wholesome as Mother Nature's herbs. With all the additives and preservatives that are contained in popular concoctions such as protein powders, energy bars, sports drinks, and commercially-prepared ephedrine supplements, athletes are putting more into their bodies than they think they are—many of the ingredients of which are harmful.

Ginseng and echinacea have both been scientifically proven to assist in athletic performance. Yerba mate and burdock are excellent herbs for athletic recovery; they both have been shown to reduce lactic acid build-up in the muscles and decrease post-workout soreness in the joints.[429]

Finally, hawthorn "supports the health and repair of ligaments, tendons, and muscles."[430]

Helpful Herbs

- Burdock
- Echinacea
- Ginseng
- Hawthorn
- Yerba mate

Athlete's Brew

Ingredients:
1 part burdock root
1 part echinacea leaf and root
2 parts hawthorn leaf, flower, and berry
8 oz. hot water

Directions:
Combine dried herbs and steep in water, covered, for 10–15 minutes.
Remove herbs from water, and sip tea slowly.

Bone Health

Horsetail is an amazing herb for bone building and repair as it directly stimulates the production of bone cells, which helps increase formation of bone tissue. Horsetail also supplies large amounts of readily absorbable calcium to the body and is rich in other minerals that the body uses to repair and rebuild injured tissue.[431] Red clover is also hypothesized to support good bone health.[432]

Milk may not do a body good, but these herbs most definitely do.

Helpful Herbs

- Horsetail
- Red clover

BONE-UP TEA

Ingredients:
1 part horsetail leaf
1 part red clover
8 oz. hot water

Directions:
Combine dried herbs and steep in water, covered, for 10–15 minutes.
Remove herbs from water, and sip tea slowly.

CANCER TREATMENT AND PREVENTION

The following herbs have all been well-researched and are notorious for containing various anticancer values and properties. For example, ginkgo is known for preventing genetic-associated reproductive cancers[433] while echinacea is widely believed to be a helpful herb to include in one's cancer-fighting program because of its ability to boost the immune system. "The University of Munich has shown that it stimulates interleukin and increases levels of white B [blood cells] and lymphocytes [the cells that can hunt down cancer cells] by 30%."[434]

Green teas display "strong anti-oxidant activity and affect several signal transduction pathways relevant to cancer development,"[435] and ginseng has been shown to be important "for treatment and prevention of breast cancer."[436] Milk thistle has been proven to fight free radicals and has "direct anticancer effects against prostate, breast, and ectocervical tumor cells."[437]

Marigold has been shown to increase cell repair and growth and to ignite the lymph system, which is crucial for increased immunity.[438] Rosehips,[439] rosemary,[440] and yarrow[441] have all been shown to possess high levels of antioxidants and are beneficial herbs to become familiar with in regards to their role in cancer prevention.

Helpful Herbs

- Echinacea
- Ginkgo
- Ginseng
- Green Tea
- Marigold
- Milk thistle
- Rosehips
- Rosemary
- Yarrow

Cancer Fighter Tea

Ingredients:
1 part echinacea leaf and root
1 part marigold flower
2 parts green tea leaf
8 oz. hot water

Directions:
Combine dried herbs and steep in water, covered, for 10–15 minutes.
Remove herbs from water, and sip tea slowly.
*Feel free to sweeten with honey or a pinch of stevia.

DETOX

A good medicinal detoxifying tea should draw out toxins and waste while simultaneously toning the liver, kidneys, and skin. The following herbs were meant for this job!

Dandelion and burdock are both amazing cleansers that strain and filter toxins from the blood and liver.[442] Dandelion "improves the function of the pancreas, spleen, stomach, and kidneys without depleting potassium from the body,"[443] and burdock "acts as a blood purifier with minimal side effects and with minimal stress to the body."[444]

For those looking for a digestive cleanse, cinnamon, licorice,[445] and fennel are all pretty amazing.

Helpful Herbs

- Burdock
- Cinnamon
- Dandelion
- Fennel
- Licorice

DETOX DRINK

Ingredients:
1 part dandelion leaf and root
1 part burdock root
8 oz. hot water

Directions:
Combine dried herbs and steep in water, covered, for 10–15 minutes.
Remove herbs from water, and sip tea slowly.

HAIR AND NAIL HEALTH

The following two herbs are successful in hair and nail restoration: horsetail is absolutely *teeming* with silica which helps increase and promote tissue, hair, and nail growth,[446] and rosemary has been shown to be beneficial in treatment of baldness, particularly when the tea is used as a scalp rinse.[447] To get rid of head lice, try the eucalyptus scalp rinse on page 27.

Helpful Herbs

- Horsetail
- Rosemary

CUPPA SILICA

Ingredients:
1 part rosemary leaf
2 parts horsetail leaf
8 oz. hot water

Directions:
Combine dried herbs and steep in water, covered, for 10–15 minutes.
Remove herbs from water, and sip tea slowly.
*To use as a scalp rinse: combine 2 tablespoons of dried rosemary with
12 ounces of hot water. Cover, and steep for 20–30 minutes. Remove
herbs, make sure the liquid isn't hot anymore, and work it into scalp. This
helps to stimulate hair follicles and prevent future hair loss.

HEART HEALTH

A healthy heart is one which pumps regularly and rhythmically, the pressure of which is strong and stable enough to supply blood (and therefore oxygen) throughout the entire body, including the extremities. Besides exercise, the herbs below are celebrated as being immensely helpful when it comes to heart health.

Rosemary has been shown to assist in circulatory blockages and stimulate the heart rate, as well as increase blood pressure,[448] while valerian is a general heart tonic.[449]

Hawthorn has been "reported to have cardio protective effects,"[450] and ginkgo "contains flavonoids that decrease capillary permeability and fragility"[451] and improves circulatory flow.[452]

Helpful Herbs

- ❧ Ginkgo
- ❧ Hawthorn
- ❧ Rosemary
- ❧ Valerian

Heart Helper Tea

Ingredients:
1 part valerian root
1 part hawthorn fruit, flower, and leaf
8 oz. hot water

Directions:
Combine dried herbs and steep in water, covered, for 10–15 minutes.
Remove herbs from water, and sip tea slowly.
*Feel free to add a cinnamon stick (bark) to increase flavor and further stimulate the cardiovascular system.

IMMUNITY

There are many herbs that have been studied and proven to be helpful in strengthening one's immune system. Echinacea is one such herb,[453] as is ginseng, "which has been extensively reported to maintain homeostasis of the immune system and to enhance resistance to illness or microbial attacks through the regulation of immune system."[454] Regular consumption of green tea has been shown to greatly benefit the immune system (as well as several other body systems),[455] and rosehips are an "excellent immune system booster."[456]

Ginkgo and St. John's wort have also displayed positive effects on increasing one's immunity.

Helpful Herbs

- Echinacea
- Ginkgo
- Ginseng
- Green Tea
- Rosehips
- St. John's wort

IMMUNITEA

Ingredients:
1 part rosehips flower
2 parts echinacea root and leaf
8 oz. hot water

Directions:
Combine dried herbs and steep in water, covered, for 10–15 minutes.
Remove herbs from water, and sip tea slowly.

KIDNEY HEALTH

The kidneys are responsible for filtering blood and producing urine composed of waste and extra fluid. Essentially, they're extremely important organs for detoxification purposes. The kidneys are directly related to the urinary tract, which is in charge of eliminating the toxins that the kidneys filter.[457]

Cranberry has been recognized for hundreds of years for its therapeutic applications regarding kidney and urinary tract health,[458] and horsetail is another herb that benefits the kidneys.[459] Raspberry, plantain,[460] and hawthorn are also excellent at strengthening kidney function.[461]

Helpful Herbs

- Cranberry
- Hawthorn
- Horsetail
- Plantain
- Raspberry

Kick-Ass Kidney Tea

Ingredients:
1 part raspberry leaf
1 part plantain leaf
2 parts cranberry fruit
8 oz. hot water

Directions:
Combine dried herbs and steep in water, covered, for 10–15 minutes.
Remove herbs from water, and sip tea slowly.

LACTATION STIMULATION

There are many herbs that have been proven safe and effective when used to stimulate and increase milk production by new mothers. These are called *galactogogues*.

A 2011 study found herbal tea made with fenugreek "significantly increased milk production in breastfeeding women."[462] It further stated that "herbal tea supplementation seems to be useful for enhancing breast milk production and facilitating infant birth weight regain in early postnatal days."[463]

Another recent study concluded that "consumption of aniseed in lactating women increases milk."[464] The following herbs fit the bill,[465] but as with all herbal use while pregnant and/or breastfeeding, one should consult with an herbalist prior to self-administering.

Helpful Herbs

- Anise
- Fennel
- Fenugreek
- Nettle

Lactation Tea

Ingredients:
1 part anise seed
1 part nettle leaf
2 parts fenugreek seed
8 oz. hot water

Directions:
Combine dried herbs and steep in water, covered, for 10–15 minutes.
Remove herbs from water, and sip tea slowly.

Liver Health

Some of the best plants for liver health are the same ones that assist in general detox cleanses. Dandelion, [466] milk thistle, and parsley[467] are all incredible liver stimulators, detoxifiers, and toners. Milk thistle takes the cake, having "been used to treat alcoholic liver disease, acute and chronic viral hepatitis and toxin-induced liver diseases."[468]

Helpful Herbs

- Dandelion
- Milk thistle
- Parsley

LOVE YOUR LIVER TEA

Ingredients:
1 part parsley leaf and stem
1 part dandelion root
2 parts milk thistle seed
8 oz. hot water

Directions:
Combine dried herbs and steep in water, covered, for 10–15 minutes.
Remove herbs from water, and sip tea slowly.

Memory

"Mild cognitive impairment (MCI) is a transitional stage between normal aging and dementia."[469] When most people are searching for medicinal plants that naturally improve memory, reaching this stage is what they're trying hard to avoid.

One of the most popular herbs used for this purpose is ginkgo, which has been found to have an encouraging and positive effect on memory on those suffering with Alzheimer's or vascular dementia.[470]

Ginseng is another well-known memory enhancer and has been found to be "clinically effective in the cognitive performance of Alzheimer's patients."[471] The strong flavonoids in parsley have a positive influence on memory and may preserve cognitive performance with aging.[472] Rosemary has also been deemed helpful to improve cognitive function.[473]

Helpful Herbs

- Ginkgo
- Ginseng
- Parsley
- Rosemary

Forget-Me-Not Tea

Ingredients:
1 part parsley leaf and stem
1 part ginseng root
2 parts ginkgo leaf
8 oz. hot water

Directions:
Combine dried herbs and steep in water, covered, for 10–15 minutes. Remove herbs from water, and sip tea slowly. Feel free to sweeten with a pinch of stevia.

SKIN HEALTH

It's been said that one can determine the general health of another simply by noting the healthful (or not-so-healthful) appearance of one's skin, hair, and nails. For example, dry skin and brittle nails could indicate chronic dehydration while yellow skin and nails could be a sign of liver disease.

Sipping your way to healthy-looking skin is a breeze with the following herbs. Marshmallow works to soothe inflamed tissue,[474] and yarrow also helps reduce skin inflammation.[475] Marigold is known for being an overall skin tonic, and horsetail lends its super silica to the body, resulting in fresh skin and strong hair. Rosemary is anti-inflammatory and enhances cellular oxygen levels,[476] thereby producing healthier-looking skin, too.

Helpful Herbs

- Horsetail
- Marigold
- Marshmallow
- Rosemary
- Thyme
- Yarrow

BEAUTYFUL TEA

𝒟

Ingredients:
1 part marigold flower
1 part marshmallow root
2 parts horsetail leaf
8 oz. hot water

Directions:
Combine dried herbs and steep in water, covered, for 10–15 minutes.
Remove herbs from water, and sip tea slowly.

Topical Treatment for Skin Health

The skin is the largest and most diverse organ on the human body. When applied topically (externally), there are a huge variety of herbs that have healing values specific to skincare. For example, when used as a compress, marigold has the ability to heal wounds, quickly improve the appearance of bruises, and help eradicate rashes and dermatitis.[477]

In a 2013 human pharmacological study, topical application of ointment containing German chamomile extract was more effective than 0.1% hydrocortisone cream in reducing inflammation.[478] Marshmallow has been shown to reduce inflammation and can be used externally for dermatitis and eczema.[479] Echinacea treats superficial wounds and inflammation,[480] and rosemary,[481] horsetail,[482] and fenugreek[483] have all been found to improve skin health by reducing swelling. (Rosemary is also antifungal.)

Index

ABOUT THE AUTHOR

Jennifer Browne is an author, magazine writer, freelance editor, and health blogger. She's also the creator of *Fresh + Fit Vancouver*, a website that provides curated lifestyle blogs for health and wellness businesses in Vancouver, BC, which is where she resides with her husband and three children. Other books by Jennifer include *Happy Healthy Gut: The Plant-Based Diet Solution to Curing IBS and Other Chronic Digestive Disorders*, *Vegetarian Comfort Foods: The Happy Healthy Gut Guide to Delicious Plant-Based Cooking*, and *Baby Nosh: Plant-Based, Gluten-Free Goodness for Baby's Food Sensitivities*.

Visit her websites at jenniferbrowne.org and freshandfitvancouver.com, and find her on Twitter: @jennifer_browne and @freshfitvan.

REFERENCES

1   Maroon, Joseph C., Jeffrey W. Bost, and Adara Maroon. "Natural Anti-Inflammatory Agents For Pain Relief." *Surgical Neurology International*, 1 (2010): 80. doi: 10.4103/2152-7806.73804.

2   Keating, Brian, Ashley Lindstrom, Mary Ellen Lynch, and Mark Blumenthal. "Sales of Tea & Herbal Tea Increase 3.6% in United States in 2014." *The Journal of the American Botanical Council*, Spring 2015, no. 105 (2015): 63.

3   Ke, Fei, Praveen Kumar Yadav, and Liu Zhan. "Herbal Medicine in the Treatment of Ulcerative Colitis." *The Saudi Journal of Gastroenterology*, 18, no. 1 (2012): 3-10. doi: 10.4103/1319-3767.91726.

4   Gladstar, Rosemary. *Medicinal Herbs: A Beginner's Guide*, 48. Storey, MA: Storey, 2012.

5   Hussain, Sarfaraj. "Patient Counseling about Herbal-Drug Interactions." *African Journal of Traditional, Complementary and Alternative Medicines*, 8, no. 5 (2011): 152-163. doi: 10.4314/ajtcam.v8i5S.8.

6   Shojaii, Asie and Mehri Abdollahi Fard. "Review of Pharmacological Properties and Chemical Constituents of Pimpinella anisum." *ISRN Pharmaceutics* (2012): 510795. doi: 10.5402/2012/510795.

7   Ibid.

8   Ibid.

9   Ibid.

10 University of Maryland Medical Center. "Bilberry." Last modified May 7, 2013. http://umm.edu/health/medical/altmed/herb/bilberry.

11 WebMD. "Bilberry." http://www.webmd.com/vitamins-supplements/ingredientmono-202-bilberry.aspx?activeingredientid=202&activeingredientname=bilberry.

12 American Cancer Society. "Black Cohosh." http://www.cancer.org/treatment/treatmentsandsideeffects/complementaryandalternativemedicine/herbsvitaminsandminerals/black-cohosh.

13 Ibid.

14 The Mayo Clinic. "Black Cohosh (Cimicifuga racemosa, Actaea racemosa)." Last modified November 1, 2013. http://www.mayoclinic.org/drugs-supplements/black-cohosh/safety/hrb-20058861.

15 Foster, Phillip. "Muscle Recovery Herbs." Livestrong. Last modified March 2, 2014. http://www.livestrong.com/article/255408-muscle-recovery-herbs/.

16 Chan, Y. S., L. N. Cheng, J. H. Wu, et al. "A Review of the Pharmacological Effects of Arctium lappa (Burdock)." *Inflammopharmacology*, 19, no. 5 (2011): 245-254. doi: 10.1007/s10787-010-0062-4.

17 University of Maryland Medical Center. "Burdock." Last modified May 7, 2013. http://umm.edu/health/medical/altmed/herb/burdock.

18 Ibid

19 "Burdock." Last modified April 2005. http://www.forevernow.net/iAnswers/rnp/fandc-rnp5391.html.

20 National Institute of Diabetes and Digestive and Kidney Diseases. "Drug Record: Chamomile (Matricaria Recutita)." Last modified April 3, 2015. http://livertox.nih.gov/Chamomile.htm.

21 Dawid-Pać, Renata. "Medicinal Plants Used in Treatment of Inflammatory Skin Diseases." *Advances in Dermatology and Allergology*, 30, no. 3 (2013): 170-177. doi: 10.5114/pdia.2013.35620.

22 Srivastava, Janmejai K., Eswar Shankar, and Sanjay Gupta. "Chamomile: A Herbal Medicine of the Past with Bright Future." *Molecular Medicine Reports*, 3, no. 6 (2010): 895-901. doi: 10.3892/mmr.2010.377.

23 National Institute of Diabetes and Digestive and Kidney Diseases. "Drug Record: Chamomile (Matricaria Recutita)." Last modified April 3, 2015. http://livertox.nih.gov/Chamomile.htm.

24 Ibid.

25 Ibid.

26 Dawid-Pać, Renata. "Medicinal Plants Used in Treatment of Inflammatory Skin Diseases." *Advances in Dermatology and Allergology*, 30, no. 3 (2013): 170-177. doi: 10.5114/pdia.2013.35620.

27 Gladstar, Rosemary. *Medicinal Herbs: A Beginner's Guide*, 125. Storey, MA: Storey, 2012.

28 Mashhadi, Nafiseh Shokri, Reza Ghiasvand, Gholamreza Askari, et al. "Influence of Ginger and Cinnamon Intake on Inflammation and Muscle Soreness Endued by Exercise in Iranian Female Athletes." *International Journal of Preventive Medicine*, 4, no. S1 (2013): S18-S22. http://ijpm.mui.ac.ir/index.php/ijpm/article/view/1113.

29 Barron, Jon. "Liver Flush Tea." Baseline of Health Foundation. Last modified April 6, 2013. http://jonbarron.org/detox/liver-flush-tea#.VMFvzEfF9aQ.

30 Brett, Jennifer. "Cramp Bark: Herbal Remedies." How Stuff Works. http://health.howstuffworks.com/wellness/natural-medicine/herbal-remedies/cramp-bark-herbal-remedies.htm.

31 Ibid.

32 Ibid.

33 Lynch, Darren M. "Cranberry for Prevention of Urinary Tract Infections." *American Family Physician*, 70, no. 11 (2004): 2175-2177. http://www.aafp.org/afp/2004/1201/p2175.html.

34 Ibid.

35 Barron, Jon. "Liver Flush Tea." Baseline of Health Foundation. Last modified April 6, 2013. http://jonbarron.org/detox/liver-flush-tea#.VMFvzEfF9aQ.

36 Carson, Tara. "Herbs to Treat Anemia." Livestrong. Last modified August 16, 2013. http://www.livestrong.com/article/292625-herbs-to-treat-anemia/.

37 Barron, Jon. "Liver Flush Tea." Baseline of Health Foundation. Last modified April 6, 2013. http://jonbarron.org/detox/liver-flush-tea#.VMFvzEfF9aQ.

38 Clare, Bevin A., Richard S. Conroy, and Kevin Spelman. "The Diuretic Effect in Human Subjects of an Extract of Taraxacum officinale Folium over a Single Day." *Journal of Alternative Complementary Medicine*, 15, no. 8 (2009): 929-934. doi: 10.1089/acm.2008.0152.

39 Hobbs, Christopher. "Herbs for PMS." Christopher Hobbs. Last modified 1998. http://www.christopherhobbs.com/library/articles-on-herbs-and-health/herbs-for-pms/.

40 Gladstar, Rosemary. *Medicinal Herbs: A Beginner's Guide*, 125. Storey, MA: Storey, 2012.

41 Stickler, Tracy. "Migraine Herbal Home Remedies from Around the World." Healthline. Last modified April 16, 2013. http://www.healthline.com/health/migraine-herbal-home-remedies-from-around-the-world#3.

42 Body Ecology. "The 9 Benefits of Dong Quai Almost No One is Aware of." http://bodyecology.com/articles/nine_benefits_of_dong_quai.php#.VM_ydZ3F9aQ.

43 Ibid.

44 Ibid.

45 Hussain, Sarfaraj. "Patient Counseling about Herbal-Drug Interactions." *African Journal of Traditional, Complementary, and Alternative Medicines*, 8, no. 5 Supplemental (2011): 152-163. doi: 10.4314/ajtcam.v8i5S.8.

46 Block, Keith I. and Mark N. Mead. "Immune System Effects of Echinacea, Ginseng, and Astragalus: A Review." *Integrative Cancer Therapies*, 2, no. 3 (2003): 247-267. doi: 10.1177/1534735403256419.

47 University of Maryland Medical Center. "Echinacea." Last modified May 7, 2013. http://umm.edu/health/medical/altmed/herb/echinacea.

48 Miller, Sandra C. "Echinacea: A Miracle Herb against Aging and Cancer? Evidence In vivo in Mice." *Evidence-Based Complementary and Alternative Medicine*, 2, no. 3 (2005): 309-314. doi: 10.1093/ecam/neh118.

49 Gladstar, Rosemary. *Medicinal Herbs: A Beginner's Guide*, 125. Storey, MA: Storey, 2012.

50 University of Maryland Medical Center. "Elder." Last modified May 7, 2013. http://umm.edu/health/medical/altmed/herb/elderberry.

51 Ibid.

52 Sayin, Ibrahim, Cemal Cingi, Faith Oghan, et al. "Complementary Therapies in Allergic Rhinitis." *ISRN Allergy*, (2013): 938751. doi: 10.1155/2013/938751.

53   University of Maryland Medical Center. "Eucalyptus." Last modified May 7, 2013. http://umm.edu/health/medical/altmed/herb/eucalyptus.

54   Ibid.

55   NYU Langone Medical Center. "Aromatherapy." http://www.med.nyu.edu/content?ChunkIID=37427.

56   Moore, Shelley. "Herb Eyebright Side Effects." Livestrong. Last modified January 27, 2015. http://www.livestrong.com/article/119916-herb-eyebright-side-effects/.

57   VitaBase. "Eyestrain." http://www.vitabase.com/tools/disorder-library/eyestrain.aspx.

58   Müller-Limmroth W. and Fröhlich H. H. "Effect of Various Phytotherapeutic Expectorants on Mucociliary Transport." *Fortschritte der Medizin*, 98, no. 3 (1980): 95-101. http://www.ncbi.nlm.nih.gov/pubmed/7364365.

59   Barron, Jon. "Liver Flush Tea." Baseline of Health Foundation. Last modified April 6, 2013. http://jonbarron.org/detox/liver-flush-tea#.VMFvzEfF9aQ.

60   Valussi, M. "Functional Foods with Digestion-Enhancing Properties." *International Journal of Food Sciences and Nutrition*, 63, no. Suppl. 1 (2012): 82-89. doi: 10.3109/09637486.2011.627841.

61   Müller-Limmroth W. and Fröhlich H. H. "Effect of Various Phytotherapeutic Expectorants on Mucociliary Transport." *Fortschritte der Medizin*, 98, no. 3 (1980): 95-101.

62   Dawid-Pać, Renata. "Medicinal Plants Used in Treatment of Inflammatory Skin Diseases." *Advances in Dermatology and Allergology*, 30, no. 3 (2013): 170-177. doi: 10.5114/pdia.2013.35620.

63   Barron, Jon. "Liver Flush Tea." Baseline of Health Foundation. Last modified April 6, 2013. http://jonbarron.org/detox/liver-flush-tea#.VMFvzEfF9aQ.

64   Srichamroen, Anchalee, Catherine J. Field, Alan B. Thomson, and Tapan K. Basu. "The Modifying Effects of Galactomannan from Canadian-Grown Fenugreek (Trigonella foenum-graecum L.) on the Glycemic and Lipidemic Status in Rats." *Journal of Clinical Biochemistry and Nutrition*, 43, no. 3 (2008): 167-174. doi: 10.3164/jcbn.2008060.

65   Dawid-Pać, Renata. "Medicinal Plants Used in Treatment of Inflammatory Skin Diseases." *Advances in Dermatology and Allergology*, 30, no. 3 (2013): 170-177. doi: 10.5114/pdia.2013.35620.

66   Heck A. M., B.A. DeWitt, and A.L. Lukes. "Potential Interactions between Alternative Therapies and Warfarin." *American Journal of Health-System Pharmacy*, 57, no. 13 (2000): 1221-1227. http://www.ncbi.nlm.nih.gov/pubmed/10902065.

67   Pareek, Anil, Manish Suthar, Garvendra S. Rathore, and Vijay Bansal. "Feverfew (Tanacetum parthenium L.): A Systematic Review." *Pharmacognosy Review*, 5, no. 9 (2011): 103-110. doi: 10.4103/0973-7847.79105.

68 Ibid.

69 Ibid.

70 Ibid.

71 Ibid.

72 Heck A. M., B. A. DeWitt, and A. L. Lukes. "Potential Interactions between Alternative Therapies and Warfarin." *American Journal of Health-System Pharmacy*, 57, no. 13 (2000): 1221-1227. http://www.ncbi.nlm.nih.gov/pubmed/10902065.

73 Pinheiro, Jr., M. N., P. M. dos Santos, Jde N. Barros, and Neto J. Cardoso. "Oral Flaxseed Oil (Linum usitatissimum) in the Treatment for Dry-Eye Sjögren's Syndrome Patients." *Arquivos Brasileiros de Oftalmologia*, 70, no. 4 (2007): 649-655. http://www.ncbi.nlm.nih.gov/pubmed/17906762.

74 Flower, Gillian, Heidi Fritz, Lynda G. Balneaves, et al. "Flax and Breast Cancer: A Systematic Review." *Integrative Cancer Therapies*, 13, no. 3 (2014): 181-192. doi: 10.1177/1534735413502076.

75 Xu, J., X. Zhou, C. Chen, et al. "Laxative Effects of Partially Defatted Flaxseed Meal on Normal and Experimental Constipated Mice." *BioMedCentral: Complementary and Alternative Medicine*, 12, no. 14 (2012): 14. doi: 10.1186/1472-6882-12-14.

76 Leake, I. "Getting to the Root of the Antiemetic Effects of Ginger." *Nature Reviews Gastroenterology & Hepatology*, 10, no. 5 (2013): 259. doi: 10.1038/nrgastro.2013.54.

77 Mashhadi, Nafiseh Shokri, Reza Ghiasvand, Gholamreza Askari, et al. "Influence of Ginger and Cinnamon Intake on Inflammation and Muscle Soreness Endued by Exercise in Iranian Female Athletes." *International Journal of Preventive Medicine*, 4, no. S1 (2013): S18-S22. http://ijpm.mui.ac.ir/index.php/ijpm/article/view/1113.

78 University of Maryland Medical Center. "Ginger." Last modified July 31, 2013. http://umm.edu/health/medical/altmed/herb/ginger.

79 Riggins, Kimberly. "Can Certain Foods Lower Blood Pressure Immediately?" Livestrong. Last Modified August 29, 2013. http://www.livestrong.com/article/342446-foods-that-lower-blood-pressure-immediately/.

80 Jiang, W., W. Qiu, Y. Wang, et al. "Ginkgo May Prevent Genetic-Associated Ovarian Cancer Risk: Multiple Biomarkers and Anticancer Pathways Induced by Ginkgolide B in BRCA1-Mutant Ovarian Epithelial Cells." *European Journal of Cancer Prevention*, 20, no. 6 (2011): 508-517. doi: 10.1097/CEJ.0b013e328348fbb7.

81 Tang, Y., Y. Xu, S. Xiong, et al. "The Effect of Ginkgo Biloba Extract on the Expression of PKCalpha in the Inflammatory Cells and the Level of IL-5 in Induced Sputum of Asthmatic Patients." *Journal of Huazhong University of Science and Technology (Medical Sciences)*, 27, no. 4 (2007): 375-380. http://link.springer.com/article/10.1007/s11596-007-0407-4.

82   Hoffman, Ronald. "Crohn's Disease and Ulcerative Colitis." Dr. Ronald Hoffman. Last modified October 4, 2013. http://drhoffman.com/article/crohns-disease-and-ulcerative-colitis-2/#sthash.ERrODHRi.dpuf.

83   Zhao, M. X., Z. H. Dong, Z. H. Yu, et al. "Effects of Ginkgo biloba Extract in Improving Episodic Memory of Patients with Mild Cognitive Impairment: A Randomized Controlled Trial." *Journal of Chinese Integrative Medicine*, 10, no. 6 (2012): 628-634.

84   Ibid.

85   Ibid.

86   Jiang, W., W. Qiu, Y. Wang, et al. "Ginkgo May Prevent Genetic-Associated Ovarian Cancer Risk: Multiple Biomarkers and Anticancer Pathways Induced by Ginkgolide B in BRCA1-Mutant Ovarian Epithelial Cells." *European Journal of Cancer Prevention*, 20, no. 6 (2011): 508-517. doi: 10.1097/CEJ.0b013e328348fbb7.

87   Lee, S. T., K. Chu, J. Y. Sim, et al. "Panax Ginseng Enhances Cognitive Performance in Alzheimer Disease." *Alzheimer Disease and Associated Disorders*, 22, no. 3 (2008): 222-226. doi: 10.1097.WAD.0b013e31816c92e6.

88   Kang, Soo-Won and Hye-Young Min. "Ginseng, the 'Immunity Boost': The Effects of Panax ginseng on Immune System." *Journal of Ginseng Research*, 36, no. 4 (2012): 354-368. doi: 10.5142/jgr.2012.36.4.354.

89   Kang, J. H., K. H. Song, J. K. Park, et al. "Ginsenoside Rp1 from Panax ginseng Exhibits Anti-Cancer Activity by Down-Regulation of the IGF-1R/Akt Pathway in Breast Cancer Cells." *Plant Foods for Human Nutrition*, 66, no. 3 (2011): 298-305. doi: 10.1007/s11130-011-0242-4.

90   Scholey, Andrew, Anastasia Ossoukhova, Lauren Owen, et al. "Effects of American Ginseng (Panax quinquefolius) on Neurocognitive Function: An Acute, Randomised, Double-Blind, Placebo-Controlled, Crossover Study." *Psychopharmacology*, 212, no. 3 (2010): 345-356. doi: 10.1007/s00213-010-1964-y.

91   Kang, Soo-Won and Hye-Young Min. "Ginseng, the 'Immunity Boost': The Effects of Panax ginseng on Immune System." *Journal of Ginseng Research*, 36, no. 4 (2012): 354-368. doi: 10.5142/jgr.2012.36.4.354.

92   Kim, Myung-Sunny, Lim Hyun-Ja, Yang Hye Jeong, et al. "Ginseng for Managing Menopause Symptoms: A Systematic Review of Randomized Clinical Trials." *Journal of Ginseng Research*, 37, no. 1 (2013): 30-36. doi: 10.5142/jgr.2013.37.30.

93   Kang, Soo-Won and Hye-Young Min. "Ginseng, the 'Immunity Boost': The Effects of Panax ginseng on Immune System." *Journal of Ginseng Research*, 36, no. 4 (2012): 354-368. doi: 10.5142/jgr.2012.36.4.354.

94   Cherney, Kristeen. "What Is Goldenseal Root Extract Used For?" Livestrong. Last modified August 16, 2013. http://www.livestrong.com/article/232434-what-is-goldenseal-root-extract-used-for/.

95 Yu, Y., Y. Deng, B. M. Lu, et al. "Green Tea Catechins: A Fresh Flavor to Anticancer Therapy." *Apoptosis*, 19, no. 1 (2014): 1-18. doi: 10.1007/s10495-013-0908-5.

96 Maroon, Joseph C., Jeffrey W. Bost, and Adara Maroon. "Natural Anti-Inflammatory Agents For Pain Relief." *Surgical Neurology International*, 1 (2010): 80. doi: 10.4103/2152-7806.73804.

97 Yu, Y., Y. Deng, B. M. Lu, et al. "Green Tea Catechins: A Fresh Flavor to Anticancer Therapy." *Apoptosis*, 19, no. 1 (2014): 1-18. doi: 10.1007/s10495-013-0908-5.

98 Bogdanski, P., J. Suliburska, M. Szulinska, et al. "Green Tea Extract Reduces Blood Pressure, Inflammatory Biomarkers, and Oxidative Stress and Improves Parameters Associated with Insulin Resistance in Obese, Hypertensive Patients." *Nutrition Research*, 32, no. 6 (2012): 421-427. doi: 10.1016/j.nutres.2012.05.007.

99 Ibid.

100 Pae, M. and D. Wu. "Immunomodulating Effects of epigallocatechin-3-gallate from Green Tea: Mechanisms and Applications." *Food & Function*, 4, no. 9 (2013): 1287-1303. doi: 10.1039/c3fo60076a.

101 Walden, Richard and Brian Tomlinson. "Chapter 16: Cardiovascular Disease." In *Herbal Medicine: Biomolecular and Clinical Aspects*, edited by I. F. F. Benzie and S. Wachtel-Galor. 2nd ed. Boca Raton: CRC Press, 2011. http://www.ncbi.nlm.nih.gov/books/NBK92767/.

102 Ibid.

103 Ibid.

104 Kidney Cares Community. "Hawthorn for Kidney Disease and Hypertension." Last modified April 18, 2013. http://www.kidney-cares.org/hypertensive-nephropathy-nutrition-recipe/1297.html.

105 Walden, Richard and Brian Tomlinson. "Chapter 16: Cardiovascular Disease." In *Herbal Medicine: Biomolecular and Clinical Aspects*, edited by I. F. F. Benzie and S. Wachtel-Galor. 2nd ed. Boca Raton: CRC Press, 2011. http://www.ncbi.nlm.nih.gov/books/NBK92767/.

106 Gladstar, Rosemary. *Medicinal Herbs: A Beginner's Guide*, 145. Storey, MA: Storey, 2012.

107 Stickler, Tracy. "Migraine Herbal Home Remedies from Around the World." Healthline. Last modified April 16, 2013. http://www.healthline.com/health/migraine-herbal-home-remedies-from-around-the-world#3.

108 Ibid.

109 Blumenthal, M. "The Complete German Commission E Monograph: Therapeutic Guide to Herbal Medicines." In *Integrative Medicine Communications*, 147. Boston: American Botanical Council, 1998.

110 Stickler, Tracy. "Migraine Herbal Home Remedies from Around the World." Healthline. Last modified April 16, 2013. http://www.healthline.com/health/migraine-herbal-home-remedies-from-around-the-world#3.

111 Bowman, Joe. "Can Hops Get Me to Sleep?" Healthline. Last modified November 7, 2014. http://www.healthline.com/health/can-hops-get-me-to-sleep.

112 Stickler, Tracy. "Migraine Herbal Home Remedies from Around the World." Healthline. Last modified April 16, 2013. http://www.healthline.com/health/migraine-herbal-home-remedies-from-around-the-world#3.

113 Homemade Medicine. "Home Remedies for Intestinal Worms." http://www.homemademedicine.com/home-remedies-intestinal-worms.html.

114 Ibid.

115 Hughes, Martin. "What Are the Benefits of the Horehound Herb?" Livestrong. Last modified January 29, 2011. http://www.livestrong.com/article/368945-what-are-the-benefits-of-the-horehound-herb/.

116 Ibid.

117 Bessa Pereira, C., P. S. Gomes, J. Costa-Rodrigues, et al. "Equisetum arvense hydromethanolic Extracts in Bone Tissue Regeneration: in vitro Osteoblastic Modulation and Antibacterial Activity." *Cell Proliferation*, 45, no. 4 (2012): 386-396. doi: 10.1111/j.1365-2184.2012.00826.x.

118 Ibid.

119 Ibid.

120 Wichtl, M., ed. "Equiseti herba—Equisetum (English translation by Norman Grainger Bisset)." *Herbal Drugs and Phyto-pharmaceuticals*, 188-191. Stuttgard: CRC Press, 1994.

121 Stickler, Tracy. "Migraine Herbal Home Remedies from Around the World." Healthline. Last modified April 16, 2013. http://www.healthline.com/health/migraine-herbal-home-remedies-from-around-the-world#3.

122 University of Maryland Medical Center. "Lavender." Last modified May 7, 2013. http://umm.edu/health/medical-reference-guide/complementary-and-alternative-medicine-guide/herb/lavender.

123 Stickler, Tracy. "Migraine Herbal Home Remedies from Around the World." Healthline. Last modified April 16, 2013. http://www.healthline.com/health/migraine-herbal-home-remedies-from-around-the-world#3.

124 Gladstar, Rosemary. *Medicinal Herbs: A Beginner's Guide*, 151. Storey, MA: Storey, 2012.

125 HerbWisdom. "Lemons (Citrus x Limon)." http://www.herbwisdom.com/herb-lemon.html.

126 Conte, A., B. Speranza, M. Sinigaglia, and M. A. Del Nobile. "Effect of Lemon Extract on Foodborne Microorganisms." *Journal of Food Protection*, 70, no. 8 (2007): 1896-1900. http://www.ncbi.nlm.nih.gov/pubmed/17803147.

127 HerbWisdom. "Lemons (Citrus x Limon)." http://www.herbwisdom.com/herb-lemon.html.

128 Goodall, Claire. "16 Home Remedies to Relieve Constipation." Everyday Roots. http://everydayroots.com/constipation-remedies.

129 Falsetto, Sharon. "Herbal Remedies for Sinus Pressure." Livestrong. Last modified January 25, 2014. http://www.livestrong.com/article/47656-herbal-remedy sinus-pressure/.

130 Ibid.

131 University of Maryland. "Lemon Balm." Last modified May 7, 2013. http://umm.edu/health/medical/altmed/herb/lemon-balm.

132 Gladstar, Rosemary. *Medicinal Herbs: A Beginner's Guide*, 157. Storey, MA: Storey, 2012.

133 Brown, D. "Licorice Root—Potential Early Intervention for Chronic Fatigue Syndrome." EnCognitive. http://www.encognitive.com/node/15023.

134 Aly, A. M., L. Al-Alousi, and H. A. Salem. "Licorice: A Possible Anti-Inflammatory and Anti-Ulcer Drug." *AAPS PharmSciTech*, 6, no. 1 (2005): E74-E82. http://www.ncbi.nlm.nih.gov/pubmed/16353966.

135 Brown, D. "Licorice Root—Potential Early Intervention for Chronic Fatigue Syndrome." EnCognitive. http://www.encognitive.com/node/15023.

136 Asha, M. K., D. Debraj, D. Prashanth, et al. "In vitro Anti-Helicobacter Pylori Activity of a Flavonoid Rich Extract of Glycyrrhiza Glabra and Its Probable Mechanisms of Action." *Journal of Ethnopharmacology*, 145, no. 2 (2013): 581-586. doi: 10.1016/j.jep.2012.11.033.

137 Ibid.

138 Ibid.

139 Heck A. M., B.A. DeWitt, and A. L. Lukes. "Potential Interactions between Alternative Therapies and Warfarin." *American Journal of Health-System Pharmacy*, 57, no. 13 (2000): 1221-1227. http://www.ncbi.nlm.nih.gov/pubmed/10902065.

140 Global Healing Center. "The Lung Cleansing Benefits of Lungwort." Last modified May 22, 2015. http://www.globalhealingcenter.com/natural-health/lung-cleansing-benefits-of-lungwort/.

141 Ibid.

142 Ibid.

143 Matić, I. Z., Z. Juanić, K. Šavikin, et al. "Chamomile and Marigold Tea: Chemical Characterization and Evaluation of Anticancer Activity." *Phytotherapy Research*, 27, no. 6 (2013): 852-858. doi: 10.1002/ptr.4807.

144 Preethi, K. C. and R. Kuttan. "Hepato and Reno Protective Action of Calendula officinalis L. Flower Extract." *Indian Journal of Experimental Biology*, 47, no. 3 (2009): 163-168. http://www.ncbi.nlm.nih.gov/pubmed/19405380.

145 Dawid-Pać, Renata. "Medicinal Plants Used in Treatment of Inflammatory Skin Diseases." *Advances in Dermatology and Allergology*, 30, no. 3 (2013): 170-177. doi: 10.5114/pdia.2013.35620.

[146] Pommier, P., F. Gomez, M. P. Sunyach, et al. "Phase III Randomized Trial Of Calendula officinalis Compared with Trolamine for the Prevention of Acute Dermatitis During Irradiation For Breast Cancer." *Journal of Clinical Oncology*, 22, no. 8 (2004): 1447-1453. http://www.ncbi.nlm.nih.gov/pubmed/15084618.

[147] Dawid-Pać, Renata. "Medicinal Plants Used in Treatment of Inflammatory Skin Diseases." *Advances in Dermatology and Allergology*, 30, no. 3 (2013): 170-177. doi: 10.5114/pdia.2013.35620.

[148] Diverticulitis Cure. "Post Diverticulitis Surgery Pain." http://diverticulitiscure.info/tag/post-diverticulitis-surgery/.

[149] Ibid.

[150] Ibid.

[151] Goodall, Claire. "3 Herbal Teas to Help Relieve a UTI." Everyday Roots. http://everydayroots.com/uti-tea-home-remedies.

[152] RXList. "Marshmallow." http://www.rxlist.com/marshmallow-page3/supplements.htm.

[153] Ibid.

[154] Bakhshaee, M., F. Jabbari, S. Hoseini, et al. "Effect of Silymarin in the Treatment of Allergic Rhinitis." *Otolaryngology: Head and Neck Surgery*, 145, no. 6 (2011): 904-909. doi: 10.1177/0194599811423504.

[155] Abenavoli, L., R. Capasso, N. Milic, and F. Capasso. "Milk Thistle in Liver Diseases: Past, Present, Future." *Phytotherapy Research*, 24, no. 10 (2010): 1423-1432. doi: 10.1002/ptr.3207.

[156] Ibid.

[157] University of Maryland Medical Center. "Milk Thistle." Last modified May 7, 2013. http://umm.edu/health/medical/altmed/herb/milk-thistle.

[158] Gholamreza, Karimi, Maryam Vahabzadeh, Parisa Lari, et al. "'Silymarin', a Promising Pharmacological Agent for Treatment of Diseases." *Iranian Journal of Basic Medical Sciences*, 14, no. 4 (2011): 308-317. http://www.ncbi.nlm.nih.gov/pmc/articles/PMC3586829/.

[159] Frazier, Thomas H., Abigail M. Stocker, Nicole A. Kershner, et al. "Treatment of Alcoholic Liver Disease." *Therapeutic Advances in Gastroenterology*, 4, no. 1 (2011): 63-81. doi: 10.1177/1756283X10378925.

[160] Gholamreza, Karimi, Maryam Vahabzadeh, Parisa Lari, et al.. "'Silymarin', a Promising Pharmacological Agent for Treatment of Diseases." *Iranian Journal of Basic Medical Sciences*, 14, no. 4 (2011): 308-317. http://www.ncbi.nlm.nih.gov/pmc/articles/PMC3586829/.

[161] Ibid.

[162] Gladstar, Rosemary. *Medicinal Herbs: A Beginner's Guide*, 172. Storey, MA: Storey, 2012.

163 University of Maryland Medical Center. "Stinging Nettle." Last modified May 7, 2013. http://umm.edu/health/medical/altmed/herb/stinging-nettle.

164 Budzynska, Katarzyna, Zoë E. Gardner, Jean-Jacques Dugoua, et al. "Systematic Review of Breastfeeding and Herbs." *Breastfeeding Medicine*, 7, no. 6 (2012): 489 503. doi: 10.1089/bfm.2011.0122.

165 Randall, C., H. Randall, F. Dobbs, et al. "Randomized Controlled Trial of Nettle Sting for Treatment of Base-Of-Thumb Pain." *Journal of the Royal Society of Medicine*, 93, no. 6 (2000): 305-309. http://www.ncbi.nlm.nih.gov/pmc/articles/PMC1298033/.

166 University of Maryland Medical Center. "Stinging Nettle." Last modified May 7, 2013. http://umm.edu/health/medical/altmed/herb/stinging-nettle.

167 Ibid.

168 Sayin, Ibrahim, Cemal Cingi, Faith Oghan, et al. "Complementary Therapies in Allergic Rhinitis." *ISRN Allergy* (2013): 938751. doi: 10.1155/2013/938751.

169 Newall, C. A., L. A. Anderson, and J. D. Phillipson, eds. *Herbal Medicines: A Guide for Health-Care Professionals*. London: The Pharmaceutical Press, 1996.

170 Bolkent S., R. Yanardag, O. Ozsoy-Sacan, and O. Karabulut-Bulan. "Effects of Parsley (Petroselinum crispum) on the Liver of Diabetic Rats: A Morphological and Biochemical Study." *Phytotherapy Research*, 18, no. 12 (2004): 996-999. http://www.ncbi.nlm.nih.gov/pubmed/15742348.

171 Vauzour, David, Katerina Vafeiadou, Ana Rodriguez-Mateo, et al. "The Neuroprotective Potential of Flavonoids: A Multiplicity of Effects." *Genes & Nutrition*, 3, no. 3-4 (2008): 115-126. doi: 10.1007/s12263-008-0091-4.

172 Goldman, Rena. "The Health Potential of Peppermint." Healthline. Last modified November 14, 2014. http://www.healthline.com/health/peppermint-health-potential#2.

173 University of Maryland Medical Center. "Peppermint." Last modified May 7, 2013. http://umm.edu/health/medical/altmed/herb/peppermint.

174 Goldman, Rena. "The Health Potential of Peppermint." Healthline. Last modified November 14, 2014. http://www.healthline.com/health/peppermint-health-potential#2.

175 University of Maryland Medical Center. "Peppermint." Last modified May 7, 2013. http://umm.edu/health/medical/altmed/herb/peppermint.

176 Mercola. "The Power of Peppermint: 21 Health Benefits Revealed." Last modified October 14, 2013. http://articles.mercola.com/sites/articles/archive/2013/10/14/peppermint-health-benefits.aspx.

177 University of Maryland Medical Center. "Peppermint." Last modified May 7, 2013. http://umm.edu/health/medical/altmed/herb/peppermint.

178 Group, Edward. "Health Benefits of Plantain Leaf." Global Healing Center. Last modified January 5, 2015. http://www.globalhealingcenter.com/natural-health/health-benefits-of-plantain-leaf/.

179 Health System University of Michigan. "Red Raspberry leaf." Last modified January 29, 2014. http://www.uofmhealth.org/health-library/hn-2154002.

180 Ibid.

181 Ghalayini I. F., M. A. Al-Ghazo, and M. N. Harfeil. "Prophylaxis and Therapeutic Effects of Raspberry Leaf (Rubus Idaeus) on Renal Stone Formation in Balb/c Mice." *International Brazilian Journal of Urology*, 37, no. 2 (2011): 259-266. http://www.ncbi.nlm.nih.gov/pubmed/21557843.

182 Ibid.

183 Gladstar, Rosemary. *Medicinal Herbs: A Beginner's Guide*, 193. Storey, MA: Storey, 2012.

184 Gladstar, Rosemary. *Medicinal Herbs: A Beginner's Guide*, 194. Storey, MA: Storey, 2012.

185 Ibid.

186 Ibid.

187 Cohen, M. "Rosehip—An Evidence Based Herbal Medicine for Inflammation and Arthritis." *Australian Family Physician*, 41, no. 7 (2012): 495-498. http://www.ncbi.nlm.nih.gov/pubmed/22762068.

188 Widén, C., A. Ekholm, M. D. Coleman, et al. "Erythrocyte Antioxidant Protection of Rosehips (Rosa spp.)" *Oxidative Medicine and Cellular Longevity* (2012): 621579. doi: 10.1155/2012/621579.

189 Progressive. "Benefits of Rose Hips." https://progressivenutritional.com/benefits-of-rose-hips/.

190 Ibid.

191 Ibid.

192 Ibid.

193 Ozcan, M. M. and J. C. Chalchat. "Chemical Composition and Antifungal Activity of Rosemary (Rosmarinus officinalis L.) Oil from Turkey." *International Journal of Food Sciences and Nutrition*, 59, no. 7-8 (2008): 691-698. doi: 10.1080/09637480701777944.

194 al-Sereiti, M. R., K. M. Abu-Amer, and P. Sen. "Pharmacology of Rosemary (Rosmarinus officinalis Linn.) and Its Therapeutic Potentials." *Indian Journal of Experimental Biology*, 37, no. 2 (1999): 124-130. http://www.ncbi.nlm.nih.gov/pubmed/10641130.

195 Yu, M. H., J. H. Choi, I. G. Chae, et al. "Suppression of LPS-Induced Inflammatory Activities by Rosmarinus officinalis L." *Food Chemistry*, 136, no. 2 (2013): 1047-1054. doi: 10.1016/j.foodchem.2012.08.085.

196 Sayorwan, Winai, Nijsiri Ruangrungsi, Teerut Piriyapunyporn, et al. "Effects of Inhaled Rosemary Oil on Subjective Feelings and Activities of the Nervous System." *Scientia Pharmaceutica*, 81, no. 2 (2013): 531-542. doi: 10.3797/scipharm.1209-05.

197   Yu, M. H., J. H. Choi, I. G. Chae, et al. "Suppression of LPS-Induced Inflammatory Activities by Rosmarinus officinalis L." *Food Chemistry*, 136, no. 2 (2013): 1047-1054. doi: 10.1016/j.foodchem.2012.08.085.

198   Pengelly A., J. Snow, S. Y. Mills, et al. "Short-Term Study on the Effects of Rosemary on Cognitive Function in an Elderly Population." *Journal of Medicinal Food*, 15, no. 1 (2012): 10-17. doi: 10.1089/jmf.2011.0005.

199   al-Sereiti, M. R., K. M. Abu-Amer, and P. Sen. "Pharmacology of Rosemary (Rosmarinus officinalis Linn.) and Its Therapeutic Potentials." *Indian Journal of Experimental Biology*, 37, no. 2 (1999): 124-130. http://www.ncbi.nlm.nih.gov/pubmed/10641130.

200   University of Maryland Medical Center. "Rosemary." Last modified May 7, 2013. http://umm.edu/health/medical/altmed/herb/rosemary.

201   Dawid-Pać, Renata. "Medicinal Plants Used in Treatment of Inflammatory Skin Diseases." *Advances in Dermatology and Allergology*, 30, no. 3 (2013): 170-177. doi: 10.5114/pdia.2013.35620.

202   University of Maryland Medical Center. "Rosemary." Last modified May 7, 2013. http://umm.edu/health/medical/altmed/herb/rosemary.

203   Sienkiewicz, M., M. Łysakowska, M. Pastuszka, et al. "The Potential of Use Basil and Rosemary Essential Oils as Effective Antibacterial Agents." *Molecules*, 18, no. 8 (2013): 9334-9351. doi: 10.3390/molecules18089334.

204   Dawid-Pać, Renata. "Medicinal Plants Used in Treatment of Inflammatory Skin Diseases." *Advances in Dermatology and Allergology*, 30, no. 3 (2013): 170-177. doi: 10.5114/pdia.2013.35620.

205   Ibid.

206   Hamidpour, Mohsen, Rafie Hamidpour, Soheila Hamidpour, and Mina Shahlari. "Chemistry, Pharmacology, and Medicinal Property of Sage (Salvia) to Prevent and Cure Illnesses such as Obesity, Diabetes, Depression, Dementia, Lupus, Autism, Heart Disease, and Cancer." *Journal of Traditional and Complementary Medicine*, 4, no. 2 (2014): 82-88. doi: 10.4103/2225-4110.130373.

207   Ibid.

208   Riggins, Kimberly. "The Uses of Sage." Livestrong. Last modified January 28, 2015. http://www.livestrong.com/article/378713-the-uses-of-sage-tea/.

209   Ibid.

210   Gladstar, Rosemary. *Medicinal Herbs: A Beginner's Guide*, 87. Storey, MA: Storey, 2012.

211   Ke, Fei, Praveen Kumar Yadev, and Liu Zhan Ju. "Herbal Medicine in the Treatment of Ulcerative Colitis." *The Saudi Journal of Gastroenterology*, 18, no. 1 (2012): 3-10. doi: 10.4103/1319-3767.91726.

212   University of Maryland Medical Center. "Slippery Elm." Last modified May 7, 2013. http://umm.edu/health/medical-reference-guide/complementary-and-alternative-medicine-guide/herb/slippery-elm.

213   Ibid.

214   Ibid.

215   McAtee, Martina. "Slippery Elm and Constipation." Livestrong. Last modified February 4, 2014. http://www.livestrong.com/article/324123-slippery-elm-constipation/.

216   Ke, Fei, Praveen Kumar Yadev, and Liu Zhan Ju. "Herbal Medicine in the Treatment of Ulcerative Colitis." *The Saudi Journal of Gastroenterology*, 18, no. 1 (2012): 3-10. doi: 10.4103/1319-3767.91726.

217   McAtee, Martina. "Slippery Elm and Constipation." Livestrong. Last modified February 4, 2014. http://www.livestrong.com/article/324123-slippery-elm-constipation/.

218   Dawid-Pać, Renata. "Medicinal Plants Used in Treatment of Inflammatory Skin Diseases." *Advances in Dermatology and Allergology*, 30, no. 3 (2013): 170-177. doi: 10.5114/pdia.2013.35620.

219   University of Maryland Medical Center. "St. John's Wort." Last modified June 24, 2013. http://umm.edu/health/medical-reference-guide/complementary-and-alternative-medicine-guide/herb/st-johns-wort.

220   Ibid.

221   Sarris, J. and D. J. Kavanagh. "Kava and St. John's Wort: Current Evidence for Use in Mood and Anxiety Disorders." *Journal of Alternative and Complementary Medicine*, 15, no. 8 (2009): 827-836. doi: 10.1089/acm.2009.0066.

222   University of Maryland Medical Center. "St. John's Wort." Last modified June 24, 2013. http://umm.edu/health/medical-reference-guide/complementary-and-alternative-medicine-guide/herb/st-johns-wort.

223   Gladstar, Rosemary. *Medicinal Herbs: A Beginner's Guide*, 199. Storey, MA: Storey, 2012.

224   Shenefelt, Philip D. "Chapter 18: Herbal Treatment for Dermatologic Disorders." In *Herbal Medicine: Biomolecular and Clinical Aspects*, edited by I. F. F. Benzie and S. Wachtel-Galor. 2nd ed. Boca Raton: CRC Press, 2011. http://www.ncbi.nlm.nih.gov/books/NBK92761/.

225   Engels, Gayle. "Thyme." EnCognitive. http://www.encognitive.com/node/15215.

226   Shenefelt, Philip D. "Chapter 18: Herbal Treatment for Dermatologic Disorders." In *Herbal Medicine: Biomolecular and Clinical Aspects*, edited by I. F. F. Benzie and S. Wachtel-Galor. 2nd ed. Boca Raton: CRC Press, 2011. http://www.ncbi.nlm.nih.gov/books/NBK92761/.

227   Ibid.

228   Ibid.

229   University of Maryland Medical Center. "Cough." Last modified May 7, 2013. http://umm.edu/health/medical-reference-guide/complementary-and-alternative-medicine-guide/condition/cough.

230 Mishra, Shikrant and Kalpana Palanivelu. "The Effect of Curcumin (turmeric) on Alzheimer's Disease: An Overview." *Annals of Indian Academy of Neurology*, 11, no. 1 (2008): 13-19. doi: 10.4103/0972-2327.40220.

231 Gladstar, Rosemary. *Medicinal Herbs: A Beginner's Guide*, 209. Storey, MA: Storey, 2012.

232 DeVries, Lynn. "Wild Yam Health Benefits." Livestrong. Last modified August 16, 2013. http://www.livestrong.com/article/116205-wild-yam-health-benefits/.

233 Vasanthi, H. R., S. Mukherjee, D. Ray, et al. "Protective Role of Air Potato (Dioscorea bulbifera) of Yam Family in Myocardial Ischemic Reperfusion Injury." *Food & Function*, 1, no. 3 (2010): 278-283. doi: 10.1039/c0fo00048e.

234 Hughes, Martin. "Herbal Muscle Relaxants for Fibromyalgia." Livestrong. Last modified August 16, 2013. http://www.livestrong.com/article/398923-herbal-muscle-relaxants-for-fibromyalgia/.

235 Price, Maria Z. "Wild Yam Powder Benefits." Livestrong. Last modified August 16, 2013. http://www.livestrong.com/article/107193-wild-yam-powder-benefits/.

236 Saeidnia, S., A. R. Gohari, N. Mokhber-Dezfuli, and F. Kiuchi. "A Review on Phytochemistry and Medicinal Properties of the Genus Achillea." *DARU Journal of Pharmaceutical Sciences*, 19, no. 3 (2011): 173-186. http://www.ncbi.nlm.nih.gov/pmc/articles/PMC3232110/.

237 Ibid.

238 Lakshmi T, R. V. Geetha, Anitha Roy, and S. Aravind Kumar. "Yarrow (Achillea Millefolium Linn.) A Herbal Medicine Plant with Broad Therapeutic use—A Review." *International Journal of Pharmaceutical Sciences Review and Research*, 9, no. 2 (2011): 136-141. http://globalresearchonline.net/journalcontents/volume9issue2/Article-022.pdf.

239 Ibid.

240 University of Maryland Medical Center. "Yarrow." Last modified May 7, 2013. http://umm.edu/health/medical/altmed/herb/yarrow

241 Saeidnia, S., A. R. Gohari, N. Mokhber-Dezfuli, and F. Kiuchi. "A Review on Phytochemistry and Medicinal Properties of the Genus Achillea." *DARU Journal of Pharmaceutical Sciences*, 19, no. 3 (2011): 173-186. http://www.ncbi.nlm.nih.gov/pmc/articles/PMC3232110/.

242 Ibid.

243 University of Maryland Medical Center. "Yarrow." Last modified May 7, 2013. http://umm.edu/health/medical/altmed/herb/yarrow

244 Lakshmi T, R. V. Geetha, Anitha Roy, and S. Aravind Kumar. "Yarrow (Achillea Millefolium Linn.) A Herbal Medicine Plant with Broad Therapeutic use—A Review." *International Journal of Pharmaceutical Sciences Review and Research*, 9, no. 2 (2011): 136-141. http://globalresearchonline.net/journalcontents/volume9issue2/Article-022.pdf.

245   Saeidnia, S., A. R. Gohari, N. Mokhber-Dezfuli, and F. Kiuchi. "A Review on Phytochemistry and Medicinal Properties of the Genus Achillea." *DARU Journal of Pharmaceutical Sciences*, 19, no. 3 (2011): 173-186. http://www.ncbi.nlm.nih.gov/pmc/articles/PMC3232110/.

246   Stickler, Tracy. "Migraine Herbal Home Remedies from Around the World." Healthline. Last modified April 16, 2013. http://www.healthline.com/health/migraine-herbal-home-remedies-from-around-the-world#3.

247   Lakshmi T, R. V. Geetha, Anitha Roy, and S. Aravind Kumar. "Yarrow (Achillea Millefolium Linn.) A Herbal Medicine Plant with Broad Therapeutic use—A Review." *International Journal of Pharmaceutical Sciences Review and Research*, 9, no. 2 (2011): 136-141. http://globalresearchonline.net/journalcontents/volume9issue2/Article-022.pdf.

248   Gladstar, Rosemary. *Medicinal Herbs: A Beginner's Guide*, 214. Storey, MA: Storey, 2012.

249   Heck C., E. G. de Mejia. "Yerba Mate Tea (Ilex paraguariensis): A Comprehensive Review on Chemistry, Health Implications, and Technological Considerations." *Journal of Food Science*, 72, no. 9 (2007): R138-R151. http://www.ncbi.nlm.nih.gov/pubmed/18034743.

250   Riggins, Kimberly. "Benefits of Yerba Mate Tea." Livestrong. Last modified September 24, 2010. http://www.livestrong.com/article/258209-benefits-of-yerba-mate-tea/.

251   Foster, Phillip. "Muscle Recovery Herbs." Livestrong. Last modified March 2, 2014. http://www.livestrong.com/article/255408-muscle-recovery-herbs/.

252   Riggins, Kimberly. "Benefits of Yerba Mate Tea." Livestrong. Last modified September 24, 2010. http://www.livestrong.com/article/258209-benefits-of-yerba-mate-tea/.

253   Ibid.

254   Ibid.

255   Block, Keith I. and Mark N. Mead. "Immune System Effects of Echinacea, Ginseng, and Astragalus: A Review." *Integrative Cancer Therapies*, 2, no. 3 (2003): 247-267. doi: 10.1177/1534735403256419.

256   Srivastava, Janmejai K., Eswar Shankar, and Sanjay Gupta. "Chamomile: A Herbal Medicine of the Past with Bright Future." *Molecular Medicine Reports*, 3, no. 6 (2010): 895-901. doi: 10.3892/mmr.2010.377.

257   de la Forêt, Rosalee. "Marshmallow Root." Learning Herbs. Last modified July 1, 2010. http://learningherbs.com/remedies-recipes/marshmallow-root/.

258   Bode, Ann M. and Zigang Dong. "Chapter 7: The Amazing and Mighty Ginger." In *Herbal Medicine: Biomolecular and Clinical Aspects*, edited by I. F. F. Benzie and S. Wachtel-Galor. Bocha Raton: CRC Press, 2011. http://www.ncbi.nlm.nih.gov/books/NBK92775/.

259   HerbWisdom. "Lemons (Citrus x Limon)." http://www.herbwisdom.com/
        herb-lemon.html.
260   Main, Emily. "Staying Healthy with 5 Essential Herbs." Organic Gardening.
        Last modified April 16, 2015. http://www.organicgardening.com/living/
        stay-healthy-5-essential-herbs.
261   Wegener, T. and K. Kraft. "Plantain (Plantago lanceolata L.): Anti-
        Inflammatory Action in Upper Respiratory Tract Infections." Wiener
        Medizinische Wochenschrift, 149, no. 8-10 (1999): 211-216. http://
        www. ncbi.nlm.nih.gov/pubmed/10483683.
262   Predy, Gerald N., Vinti Goel, Ray Lovlin, et al. "Efficacy of an Extract of North
        American Ginseng Containing Poly-Furanosyl-Pyranosyl-Saccharides for
        Preventing Upper Respiratory Tract Infections: A Randomized Controlled
        Trial." Canadian Medical Association Journal, 173, no. 9 (2005): 1043-1048.
        doi: 10.1503/cmaj.1041470.
263   University of Maryland Medical Center. "Elderberry." Last modified May 7,
        2013. http://umm.edu/health/medical/altmed/herb/elderberry.
264   Liu, Louis Wing Cheong. "Chronic Constipation: Current Treatment Options."
        Canadian Journal of Gastroenterology, 25, no. Supplemental B (2011):
        22B-28B. http://www.ncbi.nlm.nih.gov/pmc/articles/PMC3206558/.
265   McAtee, Martina. "Slippery Elm and Constipation." Livestrong. Last modified
        February 4, 2014. http://www.livestrong.com/article/324123-slippery-
        elm-constipation/.
266   Picon, Paulo D., Rafael V. Picon, Andry F. Costa, et al. "Randomized Clinical
        Trial of a Phytotherapic Compound Containing Pimpinella anisum, Foeniculum
        vulgare, Sambucus nigra, and Cassia augustifolia for Chronic Constipation."
        BMC Complementary & Alternative Medicine, 10 (2010): 17. doi: 10.1186/
        1472-6882-10-17.
267   Ibid.
268   Rodriguez-Fragoso, Lourdes, Jorge Reyes-Esparza, Scott Burchiel, et al. "Risks
        and Benefits of Commonly Used Herbal Medicines in México." Toxicology
        and Applied Pharmacology, 227, no. 1 (2008): 125-135. doi: 10.1016/
        j. taap.2007.10.005.
269   Parihar, Meenakshi, Ankit Chouhan, M. S. Harsoliya, et al. "A Review—Cough
        & Treatments." International Journal of Natural Products Research, 1, no. 1
        (2011): 9-18. http://urpjournals.com/tocjnls/21_3.pdf.
270   University of Maryland Medical Center. "Bilberry." Last modified May 7, 2013.
        http://umm.edu/health/medical/altmed/herb/bilberry.
271   The Complete Guide to Natural Healing. "Red Raspberry leaf." Last modified
        June 15, 2011. http://www.thecompleteherbalguide.com/tags/entries/
        sore-throats.

272   Shojaii, Asie and Mehri Abdollahi Fard. "Review of Pharmacological Properties and Chemical Constituents of Pimpinella anisum." *ISRN Pharmaceutics* (2012): 510795. doi: 10.5402/2012/510795.

273   Food Facts. "What is Fennel Good For?" Mercola. http://foodfacts.mercola.com/fennel.html.

274   Goldman, Rena. "The Health Potential of Peppermint." Healthline. Last modified November 14, 2014. http://www.healthline.com/health/peppermint-health-potential#2.

275   Ke, Fei, Praveen Kumar Yadav, and Liu Zhan. "Herbal Medicine in the Treatment of Ulcerative Colitis." *The Saudi Journal of Gastroenterology*, 18, no. 1 (2012): 3-10. doi: 10.4103/1319-3767.91726.

276   Lakshmi T, R. V. Geetha, Anitha Roy, and S. Aravind Kumar. "Yarrow (Achillea Millefolium Linn.) A Herbal Medicine Plant with Broad Therapeutic use—A Review." *International Journal of Pharmaceutical Sciences Review and Research*, 9, no. 2 (2011): 136-141. http://globalresearchonline.net/journalcontents/volume9issue2/Article-022.pdf.

277   Valussi M. "Functional Foods with Digestion-Enhancing Properties." *International Journal of Food Sciences and Nutrition*, 63, no. Supplemental 1 (2012): 82-89. doi: 10.3109/09637486.2011.627841.

278   Scholey, Andrew, Anastasia Ossoukhova, Lauren Owen, et al. "Effects of American Ginseng (Panax quinquefolius) on Neurocognitive Function: An Acute, Randomised, Double-Blind, Placebo-Controlled, Crossover Study." *Psychopharmacology*, 212, no. 3 (2010): 345-356. doi: 10.1007/s00213-010-1964-y.

279   Riggins, Kimberly. "Benefits of Yerba Mate Tea." Livestrong. Last modified September 24, 2010. http://www.livestrong.com/article/258209-benefits-of-yerba-mate-tea/.

280   HerbWisdom. "Lemons (Citrus x Limon)." http://www.herbwisdom.com/herb-lemon.html.

281   Pareek, Anil, Manish Suthar, Garvendra S. Rathore, and Vijay Bansal. "Feverfew (Tanacetum parthenium L.): A Systematic Review." *Pharmacognosy Review*, 5, no. 9 (2011): 103-110. doi: 10.4103/0973-7847.79105.

282   Lakshmi T, R. V. Geetha, Anitha Roy, and S. Aravind Kumar. "Yarrow (Achillea Millefolium Linn.) A Herbal Medicine Plant with Broad Therapeutic use—A Review." *International Journal of Pharmaceutical Sciences Review and Research*, 9, no. 2 (2011): 136-141. http://globalresearchonline.net/journalcontents/volume9issue2/Article-022.pdf.

283   Goldman, Rena. "The Health Potential of Peppermint." Healthline. Last modified November 14, 2014. http://www.healthline.com/health/peppermint-health-potential#2.

284 Frazier, Thomas H., Abigail M. Stocker, Nicole A. Kershner, et al. "Treatment of Alcoholic Liver Disease." *Therapeutic Advances in Gastroenterology*, 4, no. 1 (2011): 63-81. doi: 10.1177/1756283X10378925.

285 Ahlborn, Margaret L. "Plantain." Dr. Christopher's Herbal Legacy. http://www.herballegacy.com/Ahlborn_Medicinal.html.

286 Paduch, Roman, Anna Woźniak, Piotr Niedziela, and Rebert Rejdak. "Assessment of Eyebright (Euphrasia Officinalis L.) Extract Activity in Relation to Human Corneal Cells Using In Vitro Tests." *Balkan Medical Journal*, 31, no. 1 (2014): 29-36. doi: 10.5152/balkanmedj.2014.8377.

287 Falsetto, Sharon. "Herbal Remedies for Sinus Pressure." Livestrong. Last modified January 25, 2014. http://www.livestrong.com/article/47656-herbal-remedy-sinus-pressure/.

288 Sayin, Ibrahim, Cemal Cingi, Faith Oghan, et al. "Complementary Therapies in Allergic Rhinitis." *ISRN Allergy*, (2013): 938751. doi: 10.1155/2013/938751.

289 Pareek, Anil, Manish Suthar, Garvendra S. Rathore, and Vijay Bansal. "Feverfew (Tanacetum parthenium L.): A Systematic Review." *Pharmacognosy Review*, 5, no. 9 (2011): 103-110. doi: 10.4103/0973-7847.79105.

290 Stickler, Tracy. "Migraine Herbal Home Remedies from Around the World." Healthline. Last modified April 16, 2013. http://www.healthline.com/health/migraine-herbal-home-remedies-from-around-the-world#3.

291 Goldman, Rena. "The Health Potential of Peppermint." Healthline. Last modified November 14, 2014. http://www.healthline.com/health/peppermint-health-potential#2.

292 Yu, M. H., J. H. Choi, I. G. Im, et al. "Suppression of LPS-Induced Inflammatory Activities by Rosmarinus officinalis L." *Food Chemistry*, 136, no. 2 (2013): 1047-1054. doi: 10.1016/j.foodchem.2012.08.085.

293 University of Maryland Medical Center. "Slippery Elm." Last modified May 7, 2013. http://umm.edu/health/medical/altmed/herb/slippery-elm.

294 Bauer, Kara. "Acid Reflux Disease or GERD: Prevention and Natural Treatment Approaches." HealthCentral. Last modified September 10, 2012. http://www.healthcentral.com/diet-exercise/c/299905/155696/approaches/.

295 Pareek, Anil, Manish Suthar, Garvendra S. Rathore, and Vijay Bansal. "Feverfew (Tanacetum parthenium L.): A Systematic Review." *Pharmacognosy Review*, 5, no. 9 (2011): 103-110. doi: 10.4103/0973-7847.79105.

296 Stickler, Tracy. "Migraine Herbal Home Remedies from Around the World." Healthline. Last modified April 16, 2013. http://www.healthline.com/health/migraine-herbal-home-remedies-from-around-the-world#3.

297 Ibid.

298 Ibid.

299 Brett, Jennifer. "Cramp Bark: Herbal Remedies." How Stuff Works. http://health.howstuffworks.com/wellness/natural-medicine/herbal-remedies/cramp-bark-herbal-remedies.htm.

300 Mercola. "The Power of Peppermint: 21 Health Benefits Revealed." Last modified October 14, 2013. http://articles.mercola.com/sites/articles/archive/2013/10/14/peppermint-health-benefits.aspx.

301 Hughes, Martin. "Herbal Muscle Relaxants for Fibromyalgia." Livestrong. Last modified August 16, 2013. http://www.livestrong.com/article/398923-herbal-muscle-relaxants-for-fibromyalgia/.

302 Gladstar, Rosemary. *Medicinal Herbs: A Beginner's Guide*, 209. Storey, MA: Storey, 2012.

303 Shojaii, Asie and Mehri Abdollahi Fard. "Review of Pharmacological Properties and Chemical Constituents of Pimpinella anisum." *ISRN Pharmaceutics* (2012): 510795. doi: 10.5402/2012/510795.

304 Leake I. "Getting to the Root of the Antiemetic Effects of Ginger." *Nature Reviews: Gastroenterology & Hepatology*, 10, no. 5 (2013): 259. doi: 10.1038/nrgastro.2014.54.

305 Goldman, Rena. "The Health Potential of Peppermint." Healthline. Last modified November 14, 2014. http://www.healthline.com/health/peppermint-health-potential#2.

306 American Cancer Society. "Black Cohosh." http://www.cancer.org/treatment/treatmentsandsideeffects/complementaryandalternative-medicine/herbsvitaminsandminerals/black-cohosh.

307 National Institute of Diabetes and Digestive and Kidney Diseases. "Chamomile." Livertox. Last modified May 5, 2014. http://livertox.nih.gov/Chamomile.htm.

308 Brett, Jennifer. "Cramp Bark: Herbal Remedies." How Stuff Works. http://health.howstuffworks.com/wellness/natural-medicine/herbal-remedies/cramp-bark-herbal-remedies.htm.

309 Mercola. "The Power of Peppermint: 21 Health Benefits Revealed." Last modified October 14, 2013. http://articles.mercola.com/sites/articles/archive/2013/10/14/peppermint-health-benefits.aspx.

310 Gladstar, Rosemary. *Medicinal Herbs: A Beginner's Guide*, 209. Storey, MA: Storey, 2012.

311 Farokhi, Farah and Fereshteh Khaneshi. "Histophatologic Changes of Lung In Asthmatic Male Rats Treated with Hydro-Alcoholic Extract of Plantago major and Theophylline." *Avicenna Journal of Phytomedicine*, 3, no. 2 (2013): 143-151. http://www.ncbi.nlm.nih.gov/pmc/articles/PMC4075699/.

312 al-Sereiti, M. R., K. M. Abu-Amer, and P. Sen. "Pharmacology of Rosemary (Rosmarinus officinalis Linn.) and Its Therapeutic Potentials." *Indian Journal of Experimental Biology*, 37, no. 2 (1999): 124-130. http://www.ncbi.nlm.nih.gov/pubmed/10641130.

313 Global Healing Center. "The Lung Cleansing Benefits of Lungwort." Last modified May 22, 2015. http://www.globalhealingcenter.com/natural-health/lung-cleansing-benefits-of-lungwort/.

314 Moore, Shelley. "Herb Eyebright Side Effects." Livestrong. Last modified January 27 2015. http://www.livestrong.com/article/119916-herb-eyebright-side-effects/.

315 Hughes, Martin. "What Are the Benefits of the Horehound Herb?" Livestrong. Last modified January 29, 2011. http://www.livestrong.com/article/368945-what-are-the-benefits-of-the-horehound-herb/.

316 Gladstar, Rosemary. *Medicinal Herbs: A Beginner's Guide*, 171. Storey, MA: Storey, 2012.

317 Lynch, Darren M. "Cranberry for Prevention of Urinary Tract Infections." *American Family Physician*, 70, no. 11 (2004): 2175-2177. http://www.aafp.org/afp/2004/1201/p2175.html.

318 Rajasekharan, S. K., S. Ramesh, D. Bakkiyarai, et al. "Burdock Root Extracts Limit Quorum-Sensing-Controlled Phenotypes and Biofilm Architecture in Major Urinary Tract Pathogens."*Urolithiasis*, 43, no. 1 (2015): 29-40. doi: 10.1007/s00240-014-0720-x.

319 Goodall, Claire. "3 Herbal Teas to Help Relieve a UTI." Everyday Roots. http://everydayroots.com/uti-tea-home-remedies.

320 Baseline of Health Foundation. "Horsetail Herb: Remedy for Blood Clotting and More!" http://jonbarron.org/herbal-library/herbs/horsetail-herb#.VYBFFfIVhBc.

321 Wichtl, M., ed. "Equiseti herba—Equisetum (English translation by Norman Grainger Bisset)." In *Herbal Drugs and Phyto-pharmaceuticals*, 188-191. Stuttgard: CRC Press, 1994.

322 Goodall, Claire. "3 Herbal Teas to Help Relieve a UTI." Everyday Roots. http://everydayroots.com/uti-tea-home-remedies.

323 Ghalayini I. F., M. A. Al-Ghazo, and M. N. Harfeil. "Prophylaxis and Therapeutic Effects of Raspberry Leaf (Rubus Idaeus) on Renal Stone Formation in Balb/c Mice." *International Brazilian Journal of Urology*, 37, no. 2 (2011): 259-266. http://www.ncbi.nlm.nih.gov/pubmed/21557843.

324 Shenefelt, Philip D. "Chapter 18: Herbal Treatment for Dermatologic Disorders." In *Herbal Medicine: Biomolecular and Clinical Aspects*, edited by I. F. F. Benzie and S. Wachtel-Galor. 2nd ed. Boca Raton: CRC Press, 2011. http://www.ncbi.nlm.nih.gov/books/NBK92761/.

325 Goodall, Claire. "3 Herbal Teas to Help Relieve a UTI." Everyday Roots. http://everydayroots.com/uti-tea-home-remedies.

326 Wilson, Julie. "Cranberries Are Natural Antibiotic, Source of Antioxidants." Natural News. Last modified March 7, 2015. http://www.naturalnews.com/048900_cranberries_antioxidants_natural_antibiotic.html.

327 Pareek, Anil, Manish Suthar, Garvendra S. Rathore, and Vijay Bansal. "Feverfew (Tanacetum parthenium L.): A Systematic Review." *Pharmacognosy Review*, 5, no. 9 (2011): 103-110. doi: 10.4103/0973-7847.79105.

328 Homemade Medicine. "Home Remedies for Intestinal Worms." http://www. homemademedicine.com/home-remedies-intestinal-worms.html.

329 Ibid.

330 Engels, Gayle. "Thyme." EnCognitive. http://www.encognitive.com/ node/15215.

331 University of Maryland Medical Center. "Candidiasis." Last modified May 7, 2013. http://umm.edu/health/medical/altmed/condition/candidiasis.

332 Shenefelt, Philip D. "Chapter 18: Herbal Treatment for Dermatologic Disorders." In *Herbal Medicine: Biomolecular and Clinical Aspects*, edited by I. F. F. Benzie and S. Wachtel-Galor. 2nd ed. Boca Raton: CRC Press, 2011. http://www.ncbi.nlm.nih.gov/books/NBK92761/.

333 Ibid.

334 Gladstar, Rosemary. *Medicinal Herbs: A Beginner's Guide*, 65. Storey, MA: Storey, 2012.

335 DIGHerbs. "Candida Infection." http://www.digherbs.com/candida-infection. html.

336 University of Maryland Medical Center. "Candidiasis." Last modified May 7, 2013. http://umm.edu/health/medical/altmed/condition/candidiasis.

337 Martin, Corinne. "Herbal Allergy Remedies: Echinacea, Eyebright, Golden Seal and More." Mother Earth News. Last modified May 1993. http:// www.motherearthnews.com/natural-health/herbal-allergy-remedies-zmaz93amztak.aspx.

338 Falsetto, Sharon. "Herbal Remedies for Sinus Pressure." Livestrong. Last modified January 25, 2014. http://www.livestrong.com/article/47656-herbal-remedy-sinus-pressure/.

339 Pareek, Anil, Manish Suthar, Garvendra S. Rathore, and Vijay Bansal. "Feverfew (Tanacetum parthenium L.): A Systematic Review." *Pharmacognosy Review*, 5, no. 9 (2011): 103-110. doi: 10.4103/0973-7847.79105.

340 The Mayo Clinic. "Diseases and Conditions: Anemia." Last modified August 19, 2014. http://www.mayoclinic.org/diseases-conditions/anemia/basics/ symptoms/con-20026209.

341 Kidney Cares Community. "Hawthorn for Kidney Disease and Hypertension." Last modified April 18, 2013. http://www.kidney-cares.org/hypertensive-nephropathy-nutrition-recipe/1297.html.

342 Meral, I. and M. Kanter. "Effects of Nigella sativa L. and Urtica dioica L. on Selected Mineral Status and Hematological Values in CCL4-Treated Rats." *Biological Trace Element Research*, 96, no. 1-3 (2003): 263-270. http://www. ncbi.nlm.nih.gov/pubmed/14716106.

343 Carson, Tara. "Herbs to Treat Anemia." Livestrong. Last modified August 16, 2013. http://www.livestrong.com/article/292625-herbs-to-treat-anemia/.

344   The Mayo Clinic. "Diseases and Conditions: Anxiety." Last modified August 15, 2014. http://www.mayoclinic.org/diseases-conditions/anxiety/basics/definition/con-20026282.

345   Srivastava, Janmejai K., Eswar Shankar, and Sanjay Gupta. "Chamomile: A Herbal Medicine of the Past with Bright Future." *Molecular Medicine Reports*, 3, no. 6 (2010): 895-901. doi: 10.3892/mmr.2010.377.

346   University of Maryland Medical Center. "Lemon Balm." Last modified May 7, 2013. http://umm.edu/health/medical/altmed/herb/lemon-balm.

347   Bowman, Joe. "Can Hops Get Me to Sleep?" Healthline. Last modified November 7, 2014. http://www.healthline.com/health/can-hops-get-me-to-sleep.

348   McCaffrey, R., D. J. Thomas, and A. O. Kinzelman. "The Effects of Lavender and Rosemary Essential Oils on Test-Taking Anxiety among Graduate Nursing Students." *Holistic Nursing Practice*, 23, no. 2 (2009): 88-93. doi: 10.1097/HNP.0b013e3181a1100aa.

349   Gladstar, Rosemary. *Medicinal Herbs: A Beginner's Guide*, 198. Storey, MA: Storey, 2012.

350   University of Maryland Medical Center. "Yarrow." Last modified May 7, 2013. http://umm.edu/health/medical/altmed/herb/yarrow.

351   Dawid-Pać, Renata. "Medicinal Plants Used in Treatment of Inflammatory Skin Diseases." *Advances in Dermatology and Allergology*, 30, no. 3 (2013): 170-177. doi: 10.5114/pdia.2013.35620.

352   Pareek, Anil, Manish Suthar, Garvendra S. Rathore, and Vijay Bansal. "Feverfew (Tanacetum parthenium L.): A Systematic Review." *Pharmacognosy Review*, 5, no. 9 (2011): 103-110. doi: 10.4103/0973-7847.79105.

353   Mashhadi, Nafiseh Shokri, Reza Ghiasvand, Gholamreza Askari, et al. "Influence of Ginger and Cinnamon Intake on Inflammation and Muscle Soreness Endued by Exercise in Iranian Female Athletes." *International Journal of Preventive Medicine*, 4, no. S1 (2013): S18-S22. http://ijpm.mui.ac.ir/index.php/ijpm/article/view/1113.

354   Cohen, M. "Rosehip—An Evidence Based Herbal Medicine for Inflammation and Arthritis." *Australian Family Physician*, 41, no. 7 (2012): 495-498. http://www.ncbi.nlm.nih.gov/pubmed/22762068.

355   Randall, C., H. Randall, F. Dobbs, et al. "Randomized Controlled Trial of Nettle Sting for Treatment of Base-of-Thumb Pain." *Journal of the Royal Society of Medicine*, 93, no. 6 (2000): 305-309. http://www.ncbi.nlm.nih.gov/pmc/articles/PMC1298033/.

356   Hughes, Martin. "Herbal Muscle Relaxants for Fibromyalgia." Livestrong. Last modified August 16, 2013. http://www.livestrong.com/article/398923-herbal-muscle-relaxants-for-fibromyalgia/.

357 HerbaZest. "6 Herbal Remedies to Prevent Asthma Attacks and Hay Fever." http://www.herbazest.com/wellness_articles/6_herbal_remedies_to_prevent_asthma_attacks_and_hay_fever.

358 Sayin, Ibrahim, Cemal Cingi, Faith Oghan, et al. "Complementary Therapies in Allergic Rhinitis." *ISRN Allergy* (2013): 938751. doi: 10.1155/2013/938751.

359 Tang, Y., Y. Xu, S. Xiong, et al. "The Effect of Ginkgo Biloba Extract on the Expression of PKCalpha in the Inflammatory Cells and the Level of IL-5 in Induced Sputum of Asthmatic Patients." *Journal of Huazhong University of Science and Technology (Medical Sciences)*, 27, no. 4 (2007): 375-380. http://link.springer.com/article/10.1007/s11596-007-0407-4.

360 de Sousa, A. C., D. S. Alviano, A. F. Blank, et al. "Melissa officinalis L. Essential Oil: Antitumoral and Antioxidant Activities." *Journal of Pharmacy and Pharmacology*, 56, no. 5 (2004): 677-681. http://www.ncbi.nlm.nih.gov/pubmed/15142347.

361 Pareek, Anil, Manish Suthar, Garvendra S. Rathore, and Vijay Bansal. "Feverfew (Tanacetum parthenium L.): A Systematic Review." *Pharmacognosy Review*, 5, no. 9 (2011): 103-110. doi: 10.4103/0973-7847.79105.

362 Riggins, Kimberly. "Can Certain Foods Lower Blood Pressure Immediately?" Livestrong. Last modified August 29, 2013. http://www.livestrong.com/article/342446-foods-that-lower-blood-pressure-immediately/.

363 Bogdanski, P., J. Suliburska, M. Szulinska, et al. "Green Tea Extract Reduces Blood Pressure, Inflammatory Biomarkers, and Oxidative Stress and Improves Parameters Associated with Insulin Resistance in Obese, Hypertensive Patients." *Nutrition Research*, 32, no. 6 (2012): 421-427. doi: 10.1016/j.nutres.2012.05.007.

364 Walden, Richard and Brian Tomlinson. "Chapter 16: Cardiovascular Disease." In *Herbal Medicine: Biomolecular and Clinical Aspects*, edited by I. F. F. Benzie and S. Wachtel-Galor. 2nd ed. Boca Raton: CRC Press, 2011. http://www.ncbi.nlm.nih.gov/books/NBK92767/.

365 Lakshmi T, R. V. Geetha, Anitha Roy, and S. Aravind Kumar. "Yarrow (Achillea Millefolium Linn.) A Herbal Medicine Plant with Broad Therapeutic use—A Review." *International Journal of Pharmaceutical Sciences Review and Research*, 9, no. 2 (2011): 136-141. http://globalresearchonline.net/journalcontents/volume9issue2/Article-022.pdf.

366 Kang, Soo-Won and Hye-Young Min. "Ginseng, the 'Immunity Boost': The Effects of Panax ginseng on Immune System." *Journal of Ginseng Research*, 36, no. 4 (2012): 354-368. doi: 10.5142/jgr.2012.36.4.354.

367 University of Maryland Medical Center. "Burdock." Last modified May 7, 2013. http://umm.edu/health/medical/altmed/herb/burdock.

368 Hamidpour, Mohsen, Rafie Hamidpour, Soheila Hamidpour, and Mina Shahlari. "Chemistry, Pharmacology, and Medicinal Property of Sage (Salvia) to Prevent and Cure Illnesses Such as Obesity, Diabetes, Depression, Dementia, Lupus,

Autism, Heart Disease, and Cancer." *Journal of Traditional and Complementary Medicine*, 4, no. 2 (2014): 82-88. doi: 10.4103/2225-4110.130373.

369 RXList. "Marshmallow." http://www.rxlist.com/marshmallow-page3/supplements.htm.

370 Golomb, Beatrice A. and Marcella A. Evans. "Statin Adverse Effects: A Review of the Literature and Evidence for a Mitochondrial Mechanism." *American Journal of Cardiovascular Drugs*, 8, no. 6 (2008): 373-418. http://www.ncbi.nlm.nih.gov/pmc/articles/PMC2849981/.

371 University of Maryland Medical Center. "Green Tea." Last modified July 31, 2013. http://umm.edu/health/medical/altmed/herb/green-tea.

372 University of Maryland Medical Center. "Ginger." Last modified July 31, 2013. http://umm.edu/health/medical/altmed/herb/ginger.

373 University of Maryland Medical Center. "Asian Ginseng." Last modified May 7, 2013. http://umm.edu/health/medical/altmed/herb/asian-ginseng.

374 Sarris, J. and D. J. Kavanagh. "Kava and St. John's Wort: Current Evidence for Use in Mood and Anxiety Disorders." *Journal of Alternative and Complementary Medicine*, 15, no. 8 (2009): 827-836. doi: 10.1089/acm.2009.0066.

375 Kim, Myung-Sunny, Hyun-Ja Lim, Hye Jeong Yang, et al. "Ginseng for Managing Menopause Symptoms: A Systematic Review of Randomized Clinical Trials." *Journal of Ginseng Research*, 37, no. 1 (2013): 30-36. doi: 10.5142/jgr.2013.37.30.

376 Stickler, Tracy. "Migraine Herbal Home Remedies from Around the World." Healthline. Last modified April 16, 2013. http://www.healthline.com/health/migraine-herbal-home-remedies-from-around-the-world#3.

377 University of Maryland. "Lemon Balm." Last modified May 7, 2013. http://umm.edu/health/medical/altmed/herb/lemon-balm.

378 Gladstar, Rosemary. *Medicinal Herbs: A Beginner's Guide*, 146. Storey, MA: Storey, 2012.

379 Hughes, Martin. "Can Herbs Help Heal Stomach Problems & Diverticulitis?" Livestrong. Last modified August 29, 2013. http://www.livestrong.com/article/394872-herbs-that-help-heal-stomach-problems-diverticulitis/.

380 University of Maryland Medical Center. "Diverticular Disease." Last modified July 1, 2013. http://umm.edu/health/medical/altmed/condition/diverticular-disease.

381 Dawid-Pać, Renata. "Medicinal Plants Used in Treatment of Inflammatory Skin Diseases." *Advances in Dermatology and Allergology*, 30, no. 3 (2013): 170-177. doi: 10.5114/pdia.2013.35620.

382 Hoffman, Ronald. "Crohn's Disease and Ulcerative Colitis." Dr. Ronald Hoffman. Last modified October 4, 2013. http://drhoffman.com/article/crohns-disease-and-ulcerative-colitis-2/.

383 Ibid.

384 Diverticulitis Cure. "Post Diverticulitis Surgery Pain." http://diverticulitiscure. info/tag/post-diverticulitis-surgery/.

385 Riggins, Kimberly. "The Uses of Sage." Livestrong. Last modified January 28, 2015. http://www.livestrong.com/article/378713-the-uses-of-sage-tea/.

386 Cohen, M. "Rosehip—An Evidence Based Herbal Medicine for Inflammation and Arthritis." *Australian Family Physician*, 41, no. 7 (2012): 495-498. http:// www.ncbi.nlm.nih.gov/pubmed/22762068.

387 Randall, C., H. Randall, F. Dobbs, et al. "Randomized Controlled Trial of Nettle Sting for Treatment of Base-Of-Thumb Pain." *Journal of the Royal Society of Medicine*, 93, no. 6 (2000): 305-309. http://www.ncbi.nlm.nih.gov/pmc/ articles/PMC1298033/.

388 Yu, M. H., J. H. Choi, I. G. Chae, et al. "Suppression of LPS-Induced Inflammatory Activities by Rosmarinus officinalis L." *Food Chemistry*, 136, no. 2 (2013): 1047-1054. doi: 10.1016/j.foodchem.2012.08.085.

389 Aly, A. M., L. Al-Alousi, and H. A. Salem. "Licorice: A Possible Anti-Inflammatory and Anti-Ulcer Drug." *AAPS PharmSciTech*, 6, no. 1 (2005): E74-E82. http://www.ncbi.nlm.nih.gov/pubmed/16353966.

390 University of Maryland Medical Center. "Bilberry." Last modified May 7, 2013. http://umm.edu/health/medical/altmed/herb/bilberry.

391 Crohn's and Colitis Foundation of America. "Bringing to Light the Risk of Colorectal Cancer among Crohn's & Ulcerative Colitis Patients." http://www. ccfa.org/resources/risk-of-colorectal-cancer.html.

392 University of Maryland Medical Center. "Slippery Elm." Last modified May 7, 2013. http://umm.edu/health/medical/altmed/herb/slippery-elm.

393 University of Maryland Medical Center. "Bilberry." Last modified May 7, 2013. http://umm.edu/health/medical/altmed/herb/bilberry.

394 Cohen, M. "Rosehip—An Evidence Based Herbal Medicine for Inflammation and Arthritis." *Australian Family Physician*, 41, no. 7 (2012): 495-498. http:// www.ncbi.nlm.nih.gov/pubmed/22762068.

395 Dawid-Pać, Renata. "Medicinal Plants Used in Treatment of Inflammatory Skin Diseases." *Advances in Dermatology and Allergology*, 30, no. 3 (2013): 170-177. doi: 10.5114/pdia.2013.35620.

396 Ibid.

397 Srivastava, Janmejai K., Eswar Shankar, and Sanjay Gupta. "Chamomile: A Herbal Medicine of the Past with Bright Future." *Molecular Medicine Reports*, 3, no. 6 (2010): 895-901. doi: 10.3892/mmr.2010.377.

398 WebMD. "Hops." http://www.webmd.com/vitamins-supplements/ ingredientmono-856-hops.aspx?activeingredientid=856&activeingredi-entname=hops.

399 University of Maryland. "Lemon Balm." Last modified May 7, 2013. http:// umm.edu/health/medical/altmed/herb/lemon-balm.

400   Brown, D. "Licorice Root—Potential Early Intervention for Chronic Fatigue Syndrome." EnCognitive. http://www.encognitive.com/node/15023.

401   University of Maryland Medical Center. "Bilberry." Last modified May 7, 2013. http://umm.edu/health/medical/altmed/herb/bilberry.

402   Brett, Jennifer. "Cramp Bark: Herbal Remedies." How Stuff Works. http://health.howstuffworks.com/wellness/natural-medicine/herbal-remedies/cramp-bark-herbal-remedies.htm.

403   Hoffman, Ronald. "Crohn's Disease and Ulcerative Colitis." Dr. Ronald Hoffman. Last modified October 4, 2013. http://drhoffman.com/article/crohns-disease-and-ulcerative-colitis-2/.

404   Price, Maria Z. "Wild Yam Powder Benefits." Livestrong. Last modified August 16, 2013. http://www.livestrong.com/article/107193-wild-yam-powder-benefits/.

405   Hughes, Martin. "Can Herbs Help Heal Stomach Problems & Diverticulitis?" Livestrong. Last modified August 29, 2013. http://www.livestrong.com/article/394872-herbs-that-help-heal-stomach-problems-diverticulitis/.

406   University of Maryland Medical Center. "Slippery Elm." Last modified May 7, 2013. http://umm.edu/health/medical/altmed/herb/slippery-elm.

407   University of Maryland Medical Center. "Peppermint." Last modified May 7, 2013. http://umm.edu/health/medical/altmed/herb/peppermint.

408   American Cancer Society. "Black Cohosh." http://www.cancer.org/treatment/treatmentsandsideeffects/complementaryandalternative-medicine/herbsvitaminsandminerals/black-cohosh.

409   Riggins, Kimberly. "The Uses of Sage." Livestrong. Last modified January 28, 2015. http://www.livestrong.com/article/378713-the-uses-of-sage-tea/.

410   Clinical Advisor. "Wild Yam: An Herbal Remedy for Menstrual Pain and Menopause." http://www.clinicaladvisor.com/wild-yam-an-herbal-remedy-for-menstrual-pain-and-menopause/article/225458/.

411   American Cancer Society. "Black Cohosh." http://www.cancer.org/treatment/treatmentsandsideeffects/complementaryandalternative-medicine/herbsvitaminsandminerals/black-cohosh.

412   Dawid-Pać, Renata. "Medicinal Plants Used in Treatment of Inflammatory Skin Diseases." *Advances in Dermatology and Allergology*, 30, no. 3 (2013): 170-177. doi: 10.5114/pdia.2013.35620.

413   Hobbs, Christopher. "Herbs for PMS." Christopher Hobbs. Last modified 1998. http://www.christopherhobbs.com/library/articles-on-herbs-and-health/herbs-for-pms/.

414   University of Maryland Medical Center. "Stinging Nettle." Last modified May 7, 2013. http://umm.edu/health/medical/altmed/herb/stinging-nettle.

415   Lakshmi T, R. V. Geetha, Anitha Roy, and S. Aravind Kumar. "Yarrow (Achillea Millefolium Linn.) A Herbal Medicine Plant with Broad Therapeutic use—A Review." *International Journal of Pharmaceutical Sciences Review and Research*,

9, no. 2 (2011): 136-141. http://globalresearchonline.net/journalcontents/volume9issue2/Article-022.pdf.

[416] Body Ecology. "The 9 Benefits of Dong Quai Almost No One is Aware of." http://bodyecology.com/articles/nine_benefits_of_dong_quai.php#.VM_ydZ3F9aQ.

[417] Hobbs, Christopher. "Herbs for PMS." *Christopher Hobbs*. Last modified 1998. http://www.christopherhobbs.com/library/articles-on-herbs-and-health/herbs-for-pms/.

[418] Rai, D., G. Bhatia, T. Sen, and G. Palit. "Anti-Stress Effects of Ginkgo biloba and Panax ginseng: A Comparative Study." *Journal of Pharmacological Sciences*, 93, no. 4 (2003): 458-464. http://www.ncbi.nlm.nih.gov/pubmed/14737017.

[419] Ibid.

[420] Brown, D. "Licorice Root—Potential Early Intervention for Chronic Fatigue Syndrome." EnCognitive. http://www.encognitive.com/node/15023.

[421] National Institute of Diabetes and Digestive and Kidney Diseases. "Drug Record: Chamomile (Matricaria Recutita)." Last modified April 3, 2015. http://livertox.nih.gov/Chamomile.htm.

[422] Adrenal Fatigue."What is Adrenal Fatigue?" http://www.adrenalfatigue.org/what-is-adrenal-fatigue.

[423] Nippoldt, Todd B. "Is There Such a Thing as Adrenal Fatigue?" The Mayo Clinic. Last modified May 22, 2014. http://www.mayoclinic.org/diseases-conditions/addisons-disease/expert-answers/adrenal-fatigue/faq-20057906.

[424] Adrenal Fatigue."What is Adrenal Fatigue?" http://www.adrenalfatigue.org/what-is-adrenal-fatigue.

[425] Brown, D. "Licorice Root—Potential Early Intervention for Chronic Fatigue Syndrome." EnCognitive. http://www.encognitive.com/node/15023.

[426] HealthPost. "Adrenal Fatigue: Why Am I Tired All the Time?" Last modified May 13, 2013. http://blog.healthpost.co.nz/2013/adrenal-fatigue-why-am-i-tired-all-the-time/.

[427] Riggins, Kimberly. "Benefits of Yerba Mate Tea." Livestrong. Last modified September 24, 2010. http://www.livestrong.com/article/258209-benefits-of-yerba-mate-tea/.

[428] Cohen, M. "Rosehip—An Evidence Based Herbal Medicine for Inflammation and Arthritis." *Australian Family Physician*, 41, no. 7 (2012): 495-498. http://www.ncbi.nlm.nih.gov/pubmed/22762068.

[429] Foster, Phillip. "Muscle Recovery Herbs." Livestrong. Last modified March 2, 2014. http://www.livestrong.com/article/255408-muscle-recovery-herbs/.

[430] Gladstar, Rosemary. *Medicinal Herbs: A Beginner's Guide*, 146. Storey, MA: Storey, 2012.

[431] Bessa Pereira, C., P. S. Gomes, J. Costa-Rodrigues, et al. "Equisetum arvense hydromethanolic Extracts in Bone Tissue Regeneration: In vitro Osteoblastic

Modulation and Antibacterial Activity." *Cell Proliferation*, 45, no. 4 (2012): 386-396. doi: 10.1111/j.1365-2184.2012.00826.x.

432 Gladstar, Rosemary. *Medicinal Herbs: A Beginner's Guide*, 194. Storey, MA: Storey, 2012.

433 Jiang, W., W. Qiu, Y. Wang, et al. "Ginkgo May Prevent Genetic-Associated Ovarian Cancer Risk: Multiple Biomarkers and Anticancer Pathways Induced by Ginkgolide B in BRCA1-Mutant Ovarian Epithelial Cells." *European Journal of Cancer Prevention*, 20, no. 6(2011): 508-517. doi: 10.1097/CEJ.0b013e328348fbb7.

434 CancerActive. "Echinacea, the Immune Boosting Herb." http://www.canceractive.com/cancer-active-page-link.aspx?n=530.

435 Yu, Y., Y. Deng, D. M. Lu, et al. "Green Tea Catechins: A Fresh Flavor to Anticancer Therapy." *Apoptosis*, 19, no. 1 (2014): 1-18. doi: 10.1007/s10495-013-0908-5.

436 Kang, J. H., K. H. Song, J. K. Park, et al. "Ginsenoside Rp1 from Panax ginseng Exhibits Anti-Cancer Activity by Down-Regulation of the IGF-1R/Akt Pathway in Breast Cancer Cells." *Plant Foods for Human Nutrition*, 66, no. 3 (2011): 298-305. doi: 10.1007/s11130-011-0242-4.

437 PubMed Health. "Milk Thistle." National Center for Biotechnology Information. Last modified April 8, 2015. http://www.ncbi.nlm.nih.gov/pubmedhealth/PMH0032607/.

438 Gladstar, Rosemary. *Medicinal Herbs: A Beginner's Guide*, 113-114. Storey, MA: Storey, 2012.

439 Widén, C., A. Ekholm, M. D. Coleman, et al. "Erythrocyte Antioxidant Protection of Rosehips (Rosa spp.)" *Oxidative Medicine and Cellular Longevity* (2012): 621579. doi: 10.1155/2012/621579.

440 al-Sereiti, M. R., K. M. Abu-Amer, and P. Sen. "Pharmacology of Rosemary (Rosmarinus officinalis Linn.) and Its Therapeutic Potentials." *Indian Journal of Experimental Biology*, 37, no. 2 (1999): 124-130. http://www.ncbi.nlm.nih.gov/pubmed/10641130.

441 Saeidnia, S., A. R. Gohari, N. Mokhber-Dezfuli, and F. Kiuchi. "A Review on Phytochemistry and Medicinal Properties of the Genus Achillea." *DARU Journal of Pharmaceutical Sciences*, 19, no. 3 (2011): 173-186. http://www.ncbi.nlm.nih.gov/pmc/articles/PMC3232110/.

442 Lin, S. C., T. C. Chung, C. C. Lin, et al. "Hepatoprotective Effects of Arctium lappa on Carbon Tetrachloride- and Acetaminophen-Induced Liver Damage." *American Journal of Chinese Medicine*, 28, no. 2 (2000): 163-173. http://www.ncbi.nlm.nih.gov/pubmed/10999435.

443 Barron, Jon. "Liver Flush Tea." Baseline of Health Foundation. Last modified April 6, 2013. http://jonbarron.org/detox/liver-flush-tea#.VMFvzEfF9aQ.

444 Chan, Y. S., L. N. Cheng, J. H. Wu, et al. "A Review of the Pharmacological Effects of Arctium lappa (Burdock)." *Inflammopharmacology*, 19, no. 5 (2011): 245-254. doi: 10.1007/s10787-010-0062-4.

445 Asha, M. K., D. Debraj, D. Prashanth, et al. "In vitro Anti-Helicobacter Pylori Activity of a Flavonoid Rich Extract of Glycyrrhiza Glabra and Its Probable Mechanisms of Action." *Journal of Ethnopharmacology*, 145, no. 2 (2013): 581-586. doi: 10.1016/j.jep.2012.11.033.

446 Bessa Pereira, C., P. S. Gomes, J. Costa-Rodrigues, et al. "Equisetum arvense hydromethanolic Extracts in Bone Tissue Regeneration: In vitro Osteoblastic Modulation and Antibacterial Activity." *Cell Proliferation*, 45, no. 4 (2012): 386-396. doi: 10.1111/j.1365-2184.2012.00826.x.

447 Sayorwan, Winai, Nijsiri Ruangrungsi, Teerut Piriyapunyporn, et al. "Effects of Inhaled Rosemary Oil on Subjective Feelings and Activities of the Nervous System." *Scientia Pharmaceutica*, 81, no. 2 (2013): 531-542. doi: 10.3797/scipharm.1209-05.

448 al-Sereiti, M. R., K. M. Abu-Amer, and P. Sen. "Pharmacology of Rosemary (Rosmarinus officinalis Linn.) and Its Therapeutic Potentials." *Indian Journal of Experimental Biology*, 37, no. 2 (1999): 124-130. http://www.ncbi.nlm.nih.gov/pubmed/10641130.

449 Gladstar, Rosemary. *Medicinal Herbs: A Beginner's Guide*, 209. Storey, MA: Storey, 2012.

450 Walden, Richard and Brian Tomlinson. "Chapter 16: Cardiovascular Disease." In *Herbal Medicine: Biomolecular and Clinical Aspects*, edited by I. F. F. Benzie and S. Wachtel-Galor. 2nd ed. Boca Raton: CRC Press, 2011. http://www.ncbi.nlm.nih.gov/books/NBK92767/.

451 Ibid.

452 Ibid.

453 Block, Keith I. and Mark N. Mead. "Immune System Effects of Echinacea, Ginseng, and Astragalus: A Review." *Integrative Cancer Therapies*, 2, no. 3 (2003): 247-267. doi: 10.1177/1534735403256419.

454 Kang, Soo-Won and Hye-Young Min. "Ginseng, the 'Immunity Boost': The Effects of Panax ginseng on Immune System." *Journal of Ginseng Research*, 36, no. 4 (2012): 354-368. doi: 10.5142/jgr.2012.36.4.354.

455 Pae, M. and D. Wu. "Immunomodulating Effects of epigallocatechin-3-gallate from Green Tea: Mechanisms and Applications." *Food & Function*, 4, no. 9 (2013): 1287-1303. doi: 10.1039/c3fo60076a.

456 HerbWisdom. "Rose Hip." http://www.herbwisdom.com/herb-rose-hip.html.

457 National Kidney and Urologic Diseases Information Clearing House. "The Kidneys and How They Work." Last modified May 21, 2014. http://kidney.niddk.nih.gov/kudiseases/pubs/yourkidneys/#wha.

458 Lynch, Darren M. "Cranberry for Prevention of Urinary Tract Infections." *American Family Physician*, 70, no. 11 (2004): 2175-2177. http://www.aafp.org/afp/2004/1201/p2175.html.

459 Wichtl, M., ed. "Equiseti herba—Equisetum (English translation by Norman Grainger Bisset)." In *Herbal Drugs and Phyto-pharmaceuticals*, 188-191. Stuttgard: CRC Press, 1994.

460 Aziz, Sharifa Abdul, Tan Lee See, Lim Yew Kuay, et al. "In Vitro Effects of Plantago Major Extract on Urolithiasis." *The Malaysian Journal of Medical Sciences*, 12, no. 2 (2005): 22-26. http://www.ncbi.nlm.nih.gov/pmc/articles/PMC3349397/.

461 Kidney Cares Community. "Hawthorn for Kidney Disease and Hypertension." Last modified April 18, 2013. http://www.kidney-cares.org/hypertensive-nephropathy-nutrition-recipe/1297.html.

462 Budzynska, Katarzyna, Zoë E. Gardner, Jean-Jacques Dugoua, et al. "Systematic Review of Breastfeeding and Herbs." *Breastfeeding Medicine*, 7, no. 6 (2012): 489-503. doi: 10.1089/bfm.2011.0122.

463 Turkyılmaz, C., E. Onal, I. M. Hirfanoglu, et al. "The Effect of Galactagogue Herbal Tea on Breast Milk Production and Short-Term Catch-up of Birth Weight in The First Week of Life." *Journal of Alternative and Complementary Medicine*, 17, no. 2 (2011): 139-142. doi: 10.1089/acm.2010.0090.

464 Shojaii, Asie and Mehri Abdollahi Fard. "Review of Pharmacological Properties and Chemical Constituents of Pimpinella anisum." *ISRN Pharmaceutics* (2012): 510795. doi: 10.5402/2012/510795.

465 Budzynska, Katarzyna, Zoë E. Gardner, Jean-Jacques Dugoua, et al. "Systematic Review of Breastfeeding and Herbs." *Breastfeeding Medicine*, 7, no. 6 (2012): 489-503. doi: 10.1089/bfm.2011.0122.

466 Lin, S. C., T. C. Chung, C. C. Lin, et al. "Hepatoprotective Effects of Arctium lappa on Carbon Tetrachloride- and Acetaminophen-Induced Liver Damage." *American Journal of Chinese Medicine*, 28, no. 2 (2000): 163-173. http://www.ncbi.nlm.nih.gov/pubmed/10999435.

467 Plantier, Rebeca. "How Parsley Tea Cleared Up My Skin." Mind, Body, Green. Last modified January 7, 2014. http://www.mindbodygreen.com/0-12196/how-parsley-tea-cleared-up-my-skin.html.

468 Abenavoli, L., R. Capasso, N. Milic, and F. Capasso. "Milk Thistle in Liver Diseases: Past, Present, Future." *Phytotherapy Research*, 24, no. 10 (2010): 1423-1432. doi: 10.1002/ptr.3207.

469 Zhao, M. X., Z. H. Dong, Z. H. Yu, et al. "Effects of Ginkgo biloba Extract in Improving Episodic Memory of Patients with Mild Cognitive Impairment: A Randomized Controlled Trial." *Journal of Chinese Integrative Medicine*, 10, no. 6 (2012): 628-634.

470 Pasquier, Florence. "Treating Vascular Disease." *The Journal of Quality Research in Dementia*, 6. http://www.alzheimers.org.uk/site/scripts/documents_info.php?documentID=744&pageNumber=5.

471   Lee, S. T., K. Chu, J. Y. Sim, et al. "Panax Ginseng Enhances Cognitive Performance in Alzheimer Disease." *Alzheimer Disease and Associated Disorders*, 22, no. 3 (2008): 222-226. doi: 10.1097.WAD.0b013e31816c92e6.

472   Vauzour, David, Katerina Vafeiadou, Ana Rodriguez-Mateo, et al. "The Neuroprotective Potential of Flavonoids: A Multiplicity of Effects." *Genes & Nutrition*, 3, no. 3-4 (2008): 115-126. doi: 10.1007/s12263-008-0091-4.

473   Pengelly A., J. Snow, S. Y. Mills, et al. "Short-Term Study on the Effects of Rosemary on Cognitive Function in an Elderly Population." *Journal of Medicinal Food*, 15, no. 1 (2012): 10-17. doi: 10.1089/jmf.2011.0005.

474   Gladstar, Rosemary. *Medicinal Herbs: A Beginner's Guide*, 167. Storey, MA: Storey, 2012.

475   Dawid-Pać, Renata. "Medicinal Plants Used in Treatment of Inflammatory Skin Diseases." *Advances in Dermatology and Allergology*, 30, no. 3 (2013): 170-177. doi: 10.5114/pdia.2013.35620.

476   Gladstar, Rosemary. *Medicinal Herbs: A Beginner's Guide*, 84. Storey, MA: Storey, 2012.

477   Dawid-Pać, Renata. "Medicinal Plants Used in Treatment of Inflammatory Skin Diseases." *Advances in Dermatology and Allergology*, 30, no. 3 (2013): 170-177. doi: 10.5114/pdia.2013.35620.

478   Ibid.

479   Ibid.

480   Ibid.

481   Ozcan, M. M. and J. C. Chalchat. "Chemical Composition and Antifungal Activity of Rosemary (Rosmarinus officinalis L.) Oil from Turkey." *International Journal of Food ScienceS and Nutrition*, 59, no. 7-8 (2008): 691-698. doi: 10.1080/09637480701777944.

482   Bessa Pereira, C., P. S. Gomes, J. Costa-Rodrigues, et al. "Equisetum arvense hydromethanolic Extracts in Bone Tissue Regeneration: In vitro Osteoblastic Modulation and Antibacterial Activity." *Cell Proliferation*, 45, no. 4 (2012): 386-396. doi: 10.1111/j.1365-2184.2012.00826.x.

483   Dawid-Pać, Renata. "Medicinal Plants Used in Treatment of Inflammatory Skin Diseases." *Advances in Dermatology and Allergology*, 30, no. 3 (2013): 170-177. doi: 10.5114/pdia.2013.35620.